Sons of Madness

Sons of Madness

Growing Up and Older with a Mentally Ill Parent

Susan L. Nathiel

 PRAEGER

AN IMPRINT OF ABC-CLIO, LLC
Santa Barbara, California • Denver, Colorado • Oxford, England

Library of Congress Cataloging-in-Publication Data

Nathiel, Susan.
  Sons of madness : growing up and older with a mentally ill parent / Susan L. Nathiel.
    pages cm
  Includes bibliographical references and index.
  ISBN 978–1–4408–0428–1 (hardcopy : alk. paper) — ISBN 978–1–4408–0429–8 (ebook) 1. Mentally ill—Family relationships. 2. Children of the mentally ill. 3. Children of the mentally ill—Mental health. 4. Adult children of dysfunctional families—Mental health. I. Title.
  RC455.4.F3N38   2013
  362.2085—dc23   2013015380

ISBN: 978–1–4408–0428–1
EISBN: 978–1–4408–0429–8

17 16 15 14 13   1 2 3 4 5

This book is also available on the World Wide Web as an eBook.
Visit www.abc-clio.com for details.

Praeger
An Imprint of ABC-CLIO, LLC

ABC-CLIO, LLC
130 Cremona Drive, P.O. Box 1911
Santa Barbara, California 93116-1911

This book is printed on acid-free paper ∞

Manufactured in the United States of America

Contents

Preface: Sons of Madness: A Club Nobody Would Join If They Had a Choice

"Sons of Madness" is not a club anybody would join if they had a choice, and how you qualify for membership is not an easy thing to talk about. The 12 men I interviewed for this book volunteered to speak with me, challenging the stereotype that men don't want to talk about their feelings. They knew they were venturing into uncomfortable territory, some for virtually the first time: their childhood pain, confusion, shame, and helplessness.

My interest in "children of madness" has its origins in my own childhood: I was raised by a schizophrenic mother about whom I was silent for many decades. Over the years, I searched in bookstores and libraries, trying to find a book for adults who had grown up with a mentally ill parent, but even as recently as a decade ago, I found virtually nothing. I finally decided to write that book myself, including not only some of my own story but also the stories of 20 other women I interviewed. My book, *Daughters of Madness* (2007), is one of the very few collections of such stories.

Last year my publisher approached me about doing a book about "sons." My first thought was that it was a good idea but that it would be harder to find men who wanted to talk about it. My second thought was that I'd have to include the story of my older brother, who ended his own life partly because of his guilt about failing in the impossible task of helping our ill mother. He was a psychiatrist and he "knew" a lot, but we never talked about this part of our lives. I wish he had been able to talk with other men about his confusion and guilt.

This is the first book of its kind: a collection of interviews with ordinary men who have extraordinary stories to tell. The men I talked to were glad to contribute to a book that they wished had been available when they were growing up.

Considering that there are approximately 25 million people in this country with serious mental illness, and that many have children, there's remarkably little written about growing up with a mentally ill parent. With this collection of stories, I intend to open the door a little wider, to add to our understanding, and to give a voice to men whose stories would otherwise be unheard, sometimes even by their closest friends.

As a culture, we talk about mental illness more than we used to; there's no doubt the wall of stigma is beginning to come down. Depression is less shameful than it was 10 years ago, and even bipolar illness is making its way into the public discourse. Schizophrenia is still the most stigmatized of all mental illnesses. In this book you'll be reading the story of Mike, who was silent about his father's mental illness until college, when he finally told his closest friend, "My father has schizophrenia."

"You know that's genetic, right?" his friend shot back. Mike barely remembers his own reaction since he was so astounded that the word "schizophrenia" had finally come out of his mouth, to another person. Yes, these revelations are not for the fainthearted.

The stigma around mental illness affects not just the person diagnosed but everyone connected to him or her by family ties. I call it "shame by association" because many people react as though it's a contagious disease. They not only avoid the stigmatized person, but also avoid anyone connected to that person, as if irrationally afraid of some kind of psychic contamination. Stigma is like that—it makes people take a step back from you. If Mike had said that his father had cancer, his friend probably would have replied, "Man, that must be tough. How's he doing?" The response he got is code for "Are you going to be crazy too?"

As I talked to these men and heard their stories, it was clear that this stigma about mental illness had affected them in two ways. They felt shame about the illness their parent had, but because of the cultural reluctance to talk about it, they were also unintentionally isolated with their natural sadness, confusion, and anger about what was happening to their parent. As boys, they all needed more information, more attention, and more support in living with and understanding their impaired parent. These stories underline what the last 10 years of research on the psychology of boys has shown: that boys are as sensitive as girls (if not more sensitive), that boys need emotional support and help as much as girls do, and that boys' relationships are extremely important to them. As I interviewed these men, I also saw how they struggled against the "man code" of stoicism and physical and mental toughness in order to acknowledge what they felt and to speak of it with authenticity despite the inevitable shame.

The men I interviewed ranged in age from their mid-20s to their mid-60s, so the older men were raised in a time when traditional views of masculinity were more pronounced. While they spoke frankly, it was obvious that they struggled with the cultural expectation that they not cry, not express fear or confusion, and above all not appear to be shaken by the things that had happened to them or around them. These expectations hovered closely in the background. Many of the men felt they had to justify even wanting to tell me their story.

Some of them started out trying to be objective and factual (and of course there's a place for that) and were surprised to find themselves moved to tears as they remembered, and felt, more of the pain and confusion that troubled them as children. I was touched by how well and deeply they tried to answer my questions.

In some of the interviews I offered my thoughts about a diagnosis of a man's father or mother, fully aware of the pitfalls of doing so without ever meeting the parent in question. Sharing those impressions seemed to be helpful, especially when the parent had never been formally diagnosed or treated.

Most of the interviews were face-to-face, in my psychotherapy office. I had a list of questions to keep us on track, and we started at the beginning, with childhood memories, and worked our way through adolescence to adulthood. Some men lived too far away to interview this way, so we adapted the process to e-mail. I have changed each man's name and altered identifying information to protect his privacy and that of his family.

After each interview I've reflected on the interview and the parts that stand out for me, and of course you, the reader, will do the same. You might give some thought to how these stories might have been different if mental illnesses were not so stigmatized and the boys had been able to speak more freely and ask for help when they needed it.

Acknowledgments

I'm deeply grateful to the men who volunteered to be interviewed for this book. They didn't expect the process to be as painful as it sometimes was, but they stuck with it. I think they all knew that we need more books like this, more stories like theirs, and a lot less shame and silence about mental illness in the family.

I also owe a posthumous debt of gratitude to my brother, whose brief autobiography and personal notebooks I used in reconstructing his story. Thanks also to his widow, Diane, who generously shared this material with me.

Thanks to Debbie Carvalko, my editor at Praeger, who is still the fastest editor in the business. She and I simultaneously decided that *Sons* was a good idea, and the project took off quickly. My agent Linda Konner has been very helpful in this project as well as helping to find the companion book, *Daughters of Madness*, a home in the paperback world.

Thanks to all my supporters: many patients; many readers of my first book about "daughters"; many colleagues at work; my Women's Psychotherapy Group friends who regularly hear my updates, doubts, and triumphs; my long-standing breakfast club pals; and online supporters in various "children of mentally ill parents" blogs and websites. Thanks to Annita Sawyer for bringing me into the New Haven Writing Group whose members offered timely comments and suggestions. Special thanks to early readers Eric Rennie, Beth Culler, and Hedy Lipez. And special thanks to my deadline-buddy, Dianne Bouvier, with whom I exchanged hundreds of sometimes hilarious e-mails about our to-do lists and daily accomplishments as we moved toward our separate deadlines with identical dates. And thanks to my family, who always cheer me on and share in my satisfaction at doing this work.

1

Mike: "Nobody cared until my family was destroyed"

Mike is a 25-year-old whose father was diagnosed with schizophrenia before Mike was born. Mike's mother supported the family financially, while his father and grandparents took care of him until Mike was about 12. Mike's father got much worse at that point and was often actively psychotic, requiring a number of hospitalizations. Mike tells of the family silence and the lack of outside help or support. In the wake of his mother's death last year, Mike has broken his silence and is now a strong advocate for reducing the stigma regarding mental illness.

Can you start by telling me a little about your family?

I'm from Chicago, and I'm an only child. My father had been married before and had a daughter, but I didn't grow up with her and we don't have much contact. My father was diagnosed with schizophrenia in 1981, and then my parents got married in 1986 and I was born in 1987.

Did you know about your father's diagnosis early on, or is this something you know in retrospect?

From my earliest memories, I knew that our family was different because my dad didn't work. He was disabled from the time he was diagnosed with schizophrenia, and the reason he was diagnosed was because he tried to kill himself by jumping off the hospital building. That was always lingering in the background, that he had been really seriously suicidal, and he also had this chronic back condition from that time, because he was badly injured in the suicide attempt.

So I knew from the age of three that my family was different. When I was in kindergarten or preschool, he would take me to school and we spent a lot of time together. We also lived very close to both sets of grandparents, and they also took care of me quite a bit. Before I went to school, I would often spend the days with them. So I knew from very early on that I was different from my peers.

Did anyone talk to you about this? Or did you ask any questions about it?
No, nobody talked about it. Actually, when I was seven years old my father told me that he had a chemical imbalance in his brain and that he was mentally ill, and that he had attempted suicide by jumping off a building. I remember the conversation well; it was pretty shocking for a seven-year-old to hear that. I couldn't really comprehend that. I don't really know why he did it then; it seemed pretty random. I guess that day he decided it was the right time. I just really didn't know what to think, and I thought to myself, "Well, okay."

Did you tell anyone about this conversation?
Oh no, not at all. I never spoke of my dad's illness until my mom died. Really, we did not speak of it at all. We had an unspoken system at home, where I wouldn't tell my mom things that I thought would upset her, and she wouldn't tell me things that she thought would upset me. Obviously, she was working outside the home quite a bit, so a lot of things happened when she wasn't there.

So he was taking some care of you during your earlier years? And then what happened when you went to elementary school and so on? How was he doing and what was it like for you?
Until I was about 13, my dad was actually in fairly good condition. But when I was about 12 or 13, my grandmother died—that was his mother—and that put him on a downward course. Before his mother died, he was definitely in better shape, but there was always a feeling that there was something wrong with him. I would say with what I know now, that he had had more of the negative symptoms of schizophrenia, like lack of motivation, that kind of thing. But before my grandma died, I don't remember times when he was really delusional or unhinged.

What were things like in the family before that?
In those earlier years, he definitely was in a better mood a lot of the time. We took vacations and traveled together as a family; we went to church; and he would come to my baseball games. He coached my baseball team one time. He was in much better spirits. I definitely enjoyed

being around him, and we got along a lot better during that time. I know he enjoyed it too. So even though he was different, and he didn't work, we had a good relationship and I think things were pretty much okay.

What were the circumstances surrounding his mother's death? Was she ill?

My grandma died very suddenly of a brain aneurysm. Actually, all of my grandparents had died by that time when I was 12 or 13. I remember spending time with them, and obviously I liked them and they took care of me, but I don't remember being especially close to any of them because I was so young.

I don't think my dad recognized that his mother's death had such a profound effect on him. Most people with schizophrenia don't really have much insight. But it was after that that his behavior really went downhill and his illness really got much worse. In that next year he started to get really angry all the time, and there were a lot of days he wouldn't get dressed or leave the house at all.

Did either your father's or mother's family know his diagnosis? How was his not working explained, and what did the extended family know about it? They lived so close—it would be hard for them not to know what was going on.

Prior to my mom's death, her family did not even know that he had schizophrenia. It's the stigma that causes the silence, because the stigma of schizophrenia is so much greater than other mental illnesses. Like bipolar illness is more talked about and kind of more acceptable. Schizophrenia is just pretty much off-limits. Evidently, they just closed their eyes to whatever was going on and left it to me and my mom to deal with. I don't know what they thought about his not having a job and staying home all the time.

I don't think it was talked about in my dad's family much either, but of course things looked much better when his parents were alive, so maybe my uncles and aunts assumed there was no problem.

That's one of the things that really upsets me and angers me, that this huge thing was happening in my family and no one did anything about it. No one asked any questions; they all just assumed that my mother was handling everything. She did an amazing job, but it's not something that one person can handle. She didn't really get any support from anyone, including the mental health system. My dad did get a lot of treatment and medication and so forth, but there were never any meetings for us as a family or any concern from professionals about what was going on in the house. She did not get any help.

How was your dad different after his mother's death? How did that affect you and your mother?

After she died there was a lot of threatening behavior toward me. He threatened to kill me numerous times. I remember he came into my room with a baseball bat once. He pushed me into a television set one time, and he pushed my mom and me one time, and that was the only time that she was there to witness it.

I was alone with him almost all the time when these things would happen. It was always like walking on eggshells going home because I never knew what he was going to be like even though I could tell instantly what his mood was. A lot of the time he would be delusional or he would be hallucinating. He would have long conversations with his dead father, my grandfather. I don't remember him being delusional or hallucinating before my grandmother died.

The other problem was that he had had a spinal fusion from his back injury, and he was often in pain and he couldn't do any physical activity for very long. So for example if we would play catch outside, he couldn't keep it up for very long before he had to go and sit down. So there was one thing we did together that we both liked, but it just slowly petered out after a while.

Did other kids know about your dad? Did they come over or did you go to their houses?

When I was younger, other kids might come over and hang out at my house, but once I got to be a teenager, I didn't want that to happen anymore. If I did want to have kids come over, I would figure out a way where my dad wouldn't be around. I definitely didn't want kids to see him or to know that he had schizophrenia. When I was younger he would walk me to the bus stop, and he would be around in the neighborhood and so forth, and that was okay; but after my grandma died, we moved out of our house and into her house not far away, and after that time he became a recluse.

What was your mother like, and how was your relationship with her?

I got along great with my mom. She was my best friend, and she is the strongest person I've ever met in my life. I don't know how she stayed together with him for 25 years. When I was younger, they showed a lot more affection for each other, more like a normal couple. But as I got older, they seemed more distant. Not that they were hostile but just not as close as they had been before. She knew that the way he was was part of his illness, but I'm sure it was really difficult for her. She would say to him "I love you" and stuff like that, but I'm sure it was hard.

I'm struck that the only person who ever talked to you about this was your father, and he did it in an inappropriate way. Did anyone else ever say anything about it?

My mother never ever used the word "schizophrenia" to me, but she would use words like "disorder" or "illness." I'm not even sure that she knew all that much about his illness. I don't think she was included in his treatment until much later on. I remember she did say a few times that she knew he heard voices.

I think in a way I didn't want to know too much; I didn't want to know a lot about his illness. The silence really didn't help with any of that. I think my mom didn't speak of it because she didn't want me to feel that I was different or that my dad was different. Of course it didn't work out that way, and that's the price you pay for having that kind of family secret.

Did you do things outside of home that were helpful to you?

Yes, I played sports when I was younger, and then in my teenage years I started acting, and I still act now. I played hockey and baseball, and then when I was about 15, I started acting. It was always my mom who took me to these events and not my dad.

Did you take care of your dad at home while your mother was at work?

Yeah, I would come home right after school and check on how he was doing. Almost everyone with schizophrenia smokes a lot, and my dad had a three-pack-a-day habit. So I remember coming home from school and making sure that he was okay, that he was still breathing, that he hadn't set the house on fire,—things like that. All those things were a big concern to me for years.

I remember in eighth grade was the first time I remember him being hospitalized. His hospitalizations only lasted three or four days. He was talking to himself; he was angry. My mom took him to a psych unit at a hospital. I was on summer vacation so I was at home during the day, and he was screaming at himself and hallucinating. It was really terrifying. Every day coming home, coming in the door was terrifying for me. I never knew if he was going to be angry or withdrawn. If he was talking to himself, it would be very very loud, like you're having a conversation except it would be having a very loud conversation with somebody who wasn't there.

You said he also threatened you sometimes? How would that come about and what would happen?

I remember once he thought I was hiding his cigarettes and he got very very angry with me. He said he would kill me if I didn't give him his cigarettes. He had never really harmed anyone physically except himself, but he had pushed me once and pushed my mom, so I didn't really know what he would do. So I just started looking for his cigarettes and eventually he calmed down. His bursts of anger would not necessarily last all that long.

I think I might also have called my mom at work and said something. But I wouldn't have told her what was going on exactly; I might have just said, "Dad is really upset and wants me to find his cigarettes so I just wanted you to know I'm looking for them."

I guess you realized that she would know why you were calling, that it was more than just a casual comment? That you wouldn't call her at work unless things were getting kind of intense at home?

I knew from a very early age that she was under a lot of stress with this and I didn't want to do or say anything that would upset her. I didn't want to do anything to add to her burden. It was a protective system in the family—I protected her, and she protected me. That's how our family survived even though that's not really how it should work.

I just had to learn how to deal with these things on my own. From a very early age, I had to figure out how to deal with my dad. There was really no one to talk to about this. There was not one single person that I could talk to that knew what was going on. I had really bad anxiety for a long time. I was really anxious and depressed, and I didn't cope with it very well. I had a lot of anger toward my dad during those years, and I definitely wanted him not to be around. I hoped something would happen where he wouldn't be around anymore. I just wanted him removed from the picture.

Did you feel you had to tell your mom if he was getting worse? How did that all work?

When he went in the hospital, it wasn't because I said anything to her. She would kind of know when things were getting out of control and she would do what she had to do. It was her decision to make. When she came home from work, he couldn't get away with some of the things that he got away with with me. She would kind of put him in his place. She definitely was not afraid of him like I was. I never saw the woman afraid in my entire life. But if she saw that he was acting up in a certain kind of way, she would do something about it.

Did you and she talk about this even in an oblique way?

No, absolutely not. We didn't talk about it at all. Of course I would hope that they would keep him in the hospital for a long time, and sometimes I hoped that they would get divorced. But my mom was an incredibly prideful person and very stubborn, and once she made her mind up about something, that was it. She loved my dad and she took her wedding vows ridiculously seriously. Nothing would ever have broken that.

What were things like when he came home from the hospital?

He was usually a little better when he came home from the hospital, but it didn't last for very long and of course we always knew that he would be going back again. He was always supposed to be on medication, but because my mom worked, she couldn't be there all the time to make sure that he took it. And I think there were a lot of times when he didn't want to take it and of course he was a lot worse. And I certainly was not involved in his medication.

When you say he was "worse," what do you mean exactly?

His thinking was very disorganized. He couldn't verbalize what he was thinking or feeling and he dressed in a more bizarre way. When he was doing better, he liked to dress pretty nicely, but when he was doing worse, his hygiene suffered and he didn't dress as well, and sometimes he would just walk around in his underwear. And also he was in chronic pain a lot of time because of his back problems.

Were there times he embarrassed you?

Yeah, a few times. Once I was playing hockey with my friends, and he came out and he wanted to play with us. I was afraid that he would do something bizarre, but I said that he could. We played for a while, and then he got angry with me and yelled at me and asked why I didn't want him to play. I had said that he could, but I guess he picked up on the vibe. He went back in the house. My friends didn't really say anything. I really tried to keep my dad at a distance. Later when I talked to my friends after I was an adult, they said that they knew something was wrong with him but they didn't know what.

Did you have friends that you spent time with, or friends whose families you got to know? That's sometimes one way for kids to get some perspective on their own families, by hanging out with their friends' families and seeing the similarities and differences.

When I was in high school, I went on vacation with my friends and their families, and I did that a few times. I was so aware of the fact that my family was different, and I just thought, "Wow, this must be what a normal family is really like." It's something I remember, that I always really wanted to have a normal family. I really wished that I could have that. During most of my teenage years, I really did not like my dad very much and was very upset with him. I definitely wanted what the other kids had.

At that time I thought of it more as having one parent who had to do everything. I have a lot in common with my friends who were raised by a single parent. So even though my dad was physically there, he just wasn't in any condition emotionally or physically to be available to either one of us.

Did you spend time with these friends at other times?

I did hang out with friends at school, but that's as far as it went. I was just afraid of their judgment and the stigma. I never dated in high school because I was afraid to bring anyone home. It wouldn't be easy—nobody seems to know what schizophrenia is, and then I wouldn't know how my father would be on a particular day anyway. So I didn't date and I also didn't make close friends that I would have to bring home. So I was just more of a loner.

Were there other ways that you coped with how things were?

I got into acting kind of accidentally because a friend of mine was making a film when I was a teenager, and he asked if I wanted to be in it and I said yes. I enjoyed it a lot and I still enjoy it. I think it comes naturally to me 'cause I always felt like I was wearing a mask when I went out the door of my house, because nobody knew what was going on with me.

You started your acting career early!

Like if I was at home and my dad was screaming at me, I walked out the door and I would put on a happy face. Nobody would have any idea what was going on. At the time my mom died, I felt kind of like a superhero—like I had one life at home and then I would put on a different persona to be out in the world. I had this awareness of how I wanted people to see me.

At what point did you start to talk about your dad, or did you do that at all before your mom died?

I definitely did not want people to know about my dad. I was concerned that I didn't want people to know, but my dad was really uncomfortable with it too. Once he said to me, "Oh, the kids at your school know that I'm crazy," and I had to tell him that no, nobody knew.

It wasn't until late in college that I decided that I would finally confide in someone. So I told one person that I really trusted. I didn't tell them any details or any long stories about anything. I basically just said, "My dad has schizophrenia," and I didn't say anything about the suicide attempt or all the other stuff that happened. Just saying the word out loud was a big hurdle for me.

By that time I had read for hours and hours on the Internet, and I got all my information that way, because nobody had given me information before that. I was pretty surprised that I actually told somebody.

What was his reaction when you told him?

He just said, right off the bat, "You know that's genetic, right?" I said yeah. I don't know what I was supposed to do with that reaction. I think I had anticipated something a lot worse than that, like some big horrified "Oh my God!"

What was it like when it came time for you to leave home, to go off to college?

I had mixed feelings about leaving home because I was worried about my dad and worried about the burden on my mom. But I also wanted out of the chaos of living at home.

So I was worried about them, but I also wanted to escape, and my mom encouraged me to live my own life. Not that we talked about it explicitly, what might happen, because a lot of what happened I didn't tell her. I didn't want to burden her, but I was worried about what he might do.

Once I got to college, I felt a lot more freedom and I enjoyed myself. I was close enough to go home sometimes but not all the time. I had a life at college. But a part of myself was always hidden. I could never be 100 percent honest.

It affected me a lot socially. Up until I told that one friend, I still wasn't talking about it at all. So I still felt I had to act out some role and that I didn't want people to know anything about my background or my family. Also, there were some things about life I just didn't know much about because I had been such a loner when I lived at home. So I felt uncomfortable about a lot of different situations that other people were used to dealing with.

I had a lot of severe anxiety when I was a kid, and I've always felt very different socially. I didn't want people to know what a crazy life I had, so I missed out on a lot of things. I had to spend a lot of time alone, so I read a lot, that kind of thing, but not much time hanging out with other kids.

You've said that things are very different now. What happened that changed things for you?

When my mom died, that's the day everything changed. I was living back at home trying to save up some money after I finished college, and I came in the house that day and said "Hi" to my mom and my dad, and then I was tired and went up to my room. A little while after that my dad was calling me from downstairs, and I didn't really pay attention because I thought he was just saying his usual weird stuff. I also heard a thud but had no idea what that was. Then he called me "Michael"—which he never does—and he said, "Mom collapsed and she's on the floor," and I ran downstairs. I pretty much knew immediately that she was dead, although I didn't think it was her heart. I tried to move her. I was really tense and angry. The paramedics came and they couldn't help her. It was a massive heart attack. I told my dad, "She's died," and he just said, "Oh, don't say that," and he seemed kind of calm while I was in a panic.

That must have been such a huge shock to you and also to your dad.

Huge. I just couldn't believe that she just died so suddenly when she wasn't even sick. I was in shock, but when other people showed up I pretty much started talking right away. I told my uncle, my father's brother, that Dad couldn't stay by himself and that I couldn't take care of him by myself. I told him I was worried about suicide and just everything if he was on his own. I said he needed supervision. My uncle did step up, luckily, and even during my mom's wake, he was on the phone trying to find assisted living places.

How did your dad react to all this?

He didn't resist the idea of living somewhere with help. I was really surprised at that; I thought it was going to be a huge fight. He did get delusional once and told me, "Mike, they killed your mom and they're trying to put me in the nuthouse." But he's adjusted and he's doing well at the place where he lives.

So here you are, about 23 or 24 years old, your mother gone so suddenly and unexpectedly, and your father in an assisted living facility. How in the world have you coped with all this? How have you managed everything?

My uncle helped me figure out practical things like how to put the house on the market. Within a couple of months, I had cleaned out the whole place and it was sold. Now I have all the family stuff in the storage unit of my apartment.

Everything changed because—and people don't get this—after my mother died, I lost my whole family. I didn't even know where I was going to live. Not that my father was really much of a parent, but I lost my home, my family, my mother, all at one time. My life became drastically different within a couple of months. I don't have a home to go home to.

And people really don't comprehend this. They just look at me. So on top of not knowing what schizophrenia is, people I talk to just don't get how someone my age could have this kind of life right now. It's really hard to try to explain.

I can just imagine how unusual that is and how hard it is to convey to other people. Like a tidal wave hit your family and nobody can comprehend it.

It took my family being completely destroyed for anyone to say, "How are you guys doing?" I don't think anybody ever asked my mom how she was, how was she coping with things. I remember my uncle, the same one that helped me after my mom died, he tried to do some "guy" things with me a few times, but I got the feeling he was just trying to toughen me up and it didn't appeal to me. I guess they had some inkling but didn't know what to do, and my mom was extremely proud and wouldn't ever have asked for help on her own. I guess I'll never know if she rejected any kind of offer of help from Dad's family, because that would be like her to do that. But I don't think they tried very hard.

The stigma of the illness meant that we were kind of invisible. If my dad had any other serious illness, people would have helped or talked about it. If he had cancer, people would have helped, or at least acknowledged it.

All this meant that my mom carried all of this completely by herself. She had to do everything. It wasn't a healthy mutual relationship. She had to provide all the financial support. She had to hold the whole thing together.

Once she died, I had no reason to keep the secrets anymore. I also wanted people to know what kind of person my mom was. She was a hero. I know now that I'm in the field and work with schizophrenics and other mentally ill people, that I was extremely lucky to have my mom. She did everything to keep the family together, and a lot of people didn't have that. I don't know what would have happened otherwise.

What do you tell people now about your family?

I tell people my father is in assisted living, and they assume it's physical. I tell everyone what's going on now because I'm not going to keep secrets anymore. But most people don't even know what schizophrenia means. Things like "depression" or even "bipolar" are more accepted— I don't usually say this, but my personal opinion is that bipolar has become the "cool" diagnosis, because people with bipolar are seen as creative and artistic. But schizophrenia is the dirty little secret nobody wants to hear about.

I talk about it all the time now, because that's part of what I'm trying to do with my life since my mom died last year. I blame her death partly on the stress of all this and on the silence and the things that she had to handle by herself. She was only 59 years old.

My mom was a very positive person, or she always seemed to be. It was very rare that I saw her visibly stressed. So I imagine that her mask was even more of a mask than mine was. She just knew how to deal with things. I know it had a huge impact on her, but sometimes I wonder if she was even aware of some of what went on. The financial cost alone was very high. She took all of that to her grave.

What do you see in your future—or is it too soon for you to have a feeling for that? It's been quite a year for you.

I definitely have some fear and anxiety about the genetic aspect of schizophrenia, about whether I'll end up with the same illness as my dad. I know I'm not out of the woods yet. My dad was diagnosed when he was 26, and I'm 25. His daughter, my half sister, is okay. I also know that there's really nothing I can do about it; if it happens, it happens. When I'm about 30 and okay, I'll be pretty happy!

It could be that he had some symptoms before he was diagnosed, and it would be good to know that, but his family is not open to talking about it at all.

Any other thoughts about what you see for yourself in your future, personally?

Like marriage and kids? I don't know; it's hard for me to get to know women. I didn't get a lot of social experience growing up. I'd like to have a relationship, but we'll see. I don't want to have kids because of the cardiac thing as well as the mental illness. Those chances are too big to take. I don't even know how they're going to affect me yet, and it's hard to even think about passing something on to a child.

It's kind of my mission in life right now to help people be able to talk about mental illness. I just think how much better my mom would've been and how much less stressed she might've been if people were able to talk about it. So it's very important to me.

What's your relationship like with your father now?

When I visit him it feels like coming home. I'm working with other mentally ill people, and I grew up with my father, so it's kind of comforting. I'm used to it.

He seems to be better now that his meds are closely monitored and other things are looked after. We can actually have a conversation that lasts more than five minutes, so that's satisfying to both of us. He still has some delusional ideas, like he thinks I'm a professional hockey player for one of the big teams in New York. Nice delusion, I guess!

You're pretty clear on your own path for right now, then?

Definitely. The legacy for both my parents is my trying to reduce the stigma about schizophrenia. I have some of my mom's characteristics—

being responsible and trying to help other people—but I don't want to continue her silence.

I know now that things should have been different for my whole family. I'm involved in NAMI [National Alliance on Mental Illness] and I go to support groups, and I'm also in therapy. But every time I'm in one of those situations, I think my mom should be sitting here next to me. My dad should be sitting here with me. There's still some anger there.

You know, you've been through quite a lot, especially for someone so young. Are you getting that feedback from people as you're talking more?

Well, actually I get more of that reaction from strangers than I do from people in my own family. So yeah, maybe it's sinking in. I guess I've lived through a lot for someone my age.

ABOUT MIKE: MY REFLECTIONS

Mike tells his own story well, and I think he has a good handle on where he is and what he's about. He's currently in therapy and has plenty to work through. He's had quite a year since his mother's death and seems to have embraced opportunities for growth.

His decision to stop being silent about himself and his family is probably the best decision he could make, and it will give him a new foundation for building a life for himself. It's daunting, though, to imagine life at 25, not knowing whether or not you might become schizophrenic in the next few years. His advocacy on the issues of mental illness and stigma may become his career, and he certainly has the credentials and passion to do it well. I would also hope that he finds some ways to use his creativity and acting ability to have some lighthearted times too.

He and both his parents had very limited lives, centered around not only caring for his father but also keeping the secret of his illness and coping with the absence of any outside help. It's an unanswered question about whether his mother could have accessed any resources earlier, but she may have tried and been rebuffed, or she herself may have rejected some offers of help. It seems that the small efforts made by Mike's dad's family weren't enough for some reason, and Mike and his mother hunkered down and devised a coping strategy that worked in its own way, for a number of years.

Mike's resilience has two major sources, it seems to me: first, his good relationship with a caring and responsive mother, and second, his good relationship with his father for the first dozen years of his life. He clearly got enough foundation to build on, despite the later challenges. He didn't report any particular guilt about his father, and he felt free to tell me how angry he was as a teenager and how much he wished his father was "out of the picture." Because he knew the history of the illness, he didn't take on any sense of responsibility for it.

Mike's story is really incomplete without knowing his mother's story, but unfortunately that will remain a mystery. We don't know how she felt about her husband both before and after his deterioration, and there are open questions too about her family being so uninformed and unavailable. The response to a family crisis or serious illness has roots in generational patterns of avoidance or engagement, so there is undoubtedly some history that could explain her response and that of her family of origin.

WHAT CAN WE LEARN FROM MIKE'S STORY?

Mike himself knows the power of silence and stigma, and this may be the best place to flesh out the consequences of both for those who aren't familiar with them.

Being silent about something very important in your life doesn't just mean that you stop talking when the taboo topic comes up. It can become the thing that defines the borders of your life. When the silence is about a parent's mental illness, it can rapidly spread to cover a very large territory.

Mike's silence became more of a problem when he was a teenager, especially after his father became more symptomatic (when Mike was 12). In the kind of casual social situations teens often encounter—at school or around other activities—there are often comments about the family, arguments with parents, offhand comments about a more normal family life that the person with the secret can't relate to and can't join in on. It's not that teenagers sit around and discuss their families, but they do make reference to parents and siblings and family events in a way that highlights the differences between more normal families and families with significant secrets. That means that any social situation can be stressful, and conversations about something as simple as planning a sleepover or getting a ride to the mall can be loaded with emotional landmines. No, the best course of action for hiding a secret like this is to stay home, play on your computer, read, and generally play it safe. Or it might mean having a few friends and making sure you always hang out at their house, not yours.

So this silence spreads until more and more of your personal life is off-limits. Eventually, it means being silent about anything that could conceivably touch the edge of "the secret."

This is why the stigma of mental illness is such a heavy burden. The person who carries the "stigma by association"—Mike, in this case—is always aware that if the secret gets out, he can be subject to ridicule or pity, or he might simply be avoided by people who feel uncomfortable with something they don't know much about and that sounds strange and scary. The paradox is that keeping the secret also creates a kind of alienation from others, just as exposing the secret might cause alienation. Being silent starts out as a solution to the problem and ends up being a problem itself.

The second thing we can take away from Mike's story is how crucial it is to have mental health services, not just for the patient who is diagnosed but also for the family. A family group, some meetings with a family therapist, some individual meetings with a social worker—all could have helped Mike's family a lot. In addition to emotional support, there might have been some more pragmatic attention focused on the financial situation to reduce the burden on Mike's mother.

2

David: "My mother's lobotomy saved my life"

David is a middle-aged man just finishing up a degree in psychology. He's the fourth of five children from an Irish Catholic working-class family, and his parents were married for more than 50 years. David's mother was psychotic and quite violent for long stretches of time when he was growing up, and he and his siblings spent several years in an institution for children whose families could not care for them. His father, a laborer with a ninth-grade education, was a simple, devout man who prayed nightly with his children, "God bless Mommy and make her well." An additional challenge David faced was being banished from his family for many years after he came out to his parents as gay.

What's the first time you recall knowing something was wrong with your mother?

I was about three years old and I was sleeping in the room with my sisters, because we were pretty poor, and I woke up to yelling and screaming in the kitchen. I remember walking to the kitchen and seeing my mother with my father's lunch bag. She was yelling at him, "I'm getting sick! I'm going to be sick. If I don't get some help, I'm going to be sick!" Now here was a guy with a ninth-grade education and I don't think he knew what she really meant. She used to say that a lot, "I'm going to be sick." He was trying to shush her and telling her to be quiet because she would wake the kids. Maybe it was that time or another time that she grabbed my sister and put her in a baby carriage to go outside, and I remember feeling very scared of her at that time.

That's pretty frightening. What other memories do you have of her?

We always ate together as a family, and that was generally good. But once I remember she snapped at the dinner table, and she grabbed a knife and went after my brother. He was yelling at her, "You're crazy!," and then he got away and she turned on me with the knife. My older sister dove on top of me to protect me.

Another time I was about five and I was lying on the floor playing with my little toys in my little imaginary world, and she just went crazy and grabbed me by my legs from behind and started pulling me. I remember what her eyes looked like—they were just bulging—and my sister was yelling, "He's done nothing!" and trying to get me away. And she finally did.

What was done to protect you or the other kids?

Oh, my father would try to put her in a bear hug and would tell us to leave, when she got like that. Anybody who was there, who was strong enough, would try to protect us kids and try to keep her from going after people. It just all happened so explosively.

What were you told about what was wrong with her? How was it explained to you?

I just knew she was sick, and that some people outside the family knew she was sick. I think my teachers at school knew it. My dad would say, "Your mommy's sick," and I knew what that meant. I knew that people who were sick could get well. So every night we would have family prayer and he would say, "God bless this person and that person, and God make Mommy well again." He was a very simple man and just knew she was sick, but he gave me hope that things would get better.

Such a simple statement, but it carries so much meaning. If she's sick, then she can get well, and he's also conveying that it's okay to acknowledge her illness. Did you hear different things from other people either in the family or outside?

Sometimes he would say explicitly that we shouldn't talk about her to other people, like neighbors. And part of that might have been that my mother's entire family blamed him for my mother's illness. Their theory was that he had made her have five kids and had "overworked her." That's why they would never help him with us kids when my mother was in the hospital.

That's kind of an odd idea considering that having five children was pretty common for Catholic families at that time. What do you recall about her being in the hospital? Were there times you visited her there or were you too young?

I would wait in the car if I was too young to go in, and I would see Mommy waving from the hospital window, and I would wait for my father or maybe my father and my sister to come back to the car. My father actually wanted to protect us from certain things—not from knowing "Mommy was sick" but from seeing too much. He would say, "Don't look at this" or "Don't listen to this, you're just a child." So I'm grateful I didn't go into the hospital then, although I did many years later, just to see what it was like.

So your mother's family didn't get involved with helping? Did they really have the view that your father had made your mother sick, so therefore they weren't going to help him or the kids?

When my mother was 16, her mother had taken her to a psychiatrist. This would be around the late 1940s. They didn't really know what was wrong with her, but the psychiatrist told her mother that once her daughter got married, she would be fine. My mother was evidently acting disturbed enough that my grandmother, an uneducated working-class woman with very little money, took her to see a psychiatrist. She was certainly not one to be going to see this kind of a doctor at all. So blaming my father didn't make all that much sense.

Did anything happen to change their view about your father?

When I was about five or so, my grandmother had come over and every-body was sitting at the table. I was between the table and the wall, and I could see a look on my mother's face that I had seen before. She was just staring into space like she would do for hours. Keep in mind that she had already had a couple of psychotic breaks and gotten violent. Then from absolutely nothing, my mother erupted and everything went flying.

So my grandmother started screaming; my father was bear-hugging my mother without hurting her, just trying to control her, and he yelled at us to "Get out." I dove under the table and froze, and my grandmother was yell-ing at me to come out from under the table and she grabbed me by the legs. I couldn't move, but I told her, "We have to get out, we have to get out," and she finally picked me up and we ran out of the house.

After that my grandmother saw that it wasn't anything he did, that it came out of absolutely nowhere. And it always happened that way. I don't think she had ever seen how madness happens really—it can come just from silence and then just explodes into the world.

So from there she took us to her house and fed us something. My mother was taken away to the hospital, and I had no idea of what was going to happen to us from then on. My grandmother didn't blame my father any-more, but other relatives still did, and there wasn't much help from them.

And what happened from that time when she was hospitalized?

My little sister and I weren't old enough to be in school, and there was nobody to watch us while my father was at work, so we were going to be placed somewhere. But my uncle was a priest and he had pull, so he arranged for us to go to a Catholic place. All of us kids went, during the week, and then came home on the weekends when my father was there. But we were all separated by age and gender, so my siblings were all there but we didn't see each other.

After a couple of years, my mother had her first lobotomy. And it was frightening for me because of what I had been told about it. I know I was maybe six or seven years old and I was in first grade, and the teacher was saying to the class, "Well, does anyone have anything they want to tell us today?" So I stood up and said, "My mother might die today." And my teacher said, "What did you say, David?" And I said it again, "My mother might die today." Because that's what I had been told. The poor woman didn't know what to say. Finally, she just went to the black-board and wrote, "Let's hope that David's mother gets well today." She was very kind.

Do you know how it came about that they decided to do a lobotomy?

I know now that my mother had gone through all known treatments, all known medications at that time. And she had been suicidal. I know she had a couple of suicide attempts that I can recall. We're talking 1963 and there really wasn't any other alternative. There were no options left. I asked my father once how he made the decision about the first lobotomy, and he said, "The doctor said it would take pressure off of her brain."

Do you think he was still optimistic about her getting better? This would have been a very tough time with her being in the hospital for such a long time, with nothing working to help her.

He only questioned whether he could have done more. He was very reli-gious and I think he was probably still hopeful. It's hard to tell what he really understood about her illness and the various things they tried. He didn't talk much, and he certainly wouldn't have asked the doctors a lot of questions.

You said "the first lobotomy"—was there another one? I didn't know people had more than one lobotomy.

I've done a lot of reading on it. Evidently, some tissue can regrow in the brain, and a lot of people—I forget the percentage—had more than one lobotomy. My mother had three over the course of those years, from when

I was about 7 to about 12 or so. I don't think the first one was that effective because she was still in the hospital afterwards.

What was that time like for you, in the Catholic institution?

I withdrew. I withdrew to such an extent that I would remain silent for weeks at a time. That became a coping mechanism for me. If I was quiet for too long, they would call my older sister and have her come talk to me. And she would say to me, "You have to talk; they're getting worried about you." Eventually, it turned out to be my way of getting her to come. She was in the older kids' area and they would bring her to see me.

I remember there was this really long hall that I would go down, and there would be some little rocking chairs for young children and I would sit in one of the rocking chairs. And there would be music for children, like "The Farmer in the Dell," so I would rock in that little chair listening to music for hours. And then one day something happened to the music and it just stopped. And I remember just sitting there in the quiet. I really thought the music was gone forever. If a little kid can be in despair, then I was in despair.

And then this woman appeared, a tall woman with long brown hair who worked there. I was silent, but she kept asking me what was wrong, and finally I said, "The music doesn't play anymore." And she picked me up and took me to another room—maybe her office, I don't recall. But she was very nice.

That was one of the times that I felt so alone, but every time that happened to me there would be someone who would come along and let me know that I wasn't alone. And I remember each one of those moments. This was one. I'm very grateful for that. To this day I can literally smell her hair, even though I can't remember what she looked like. It was the same with the teacher in school when I thought my mother might die that day.

Were there other times when the people at the institution were kind or helpful?

Listen, I'm totally not religious and I haven't been for a long time. And I know that the Catholic Church has done a lot of bad things. But nobody ever talks about the good the Church does. Those nuns really helped me and a lot of the other people at that institution.

When I was there I would sometimes wet the bed, and I would lay on the floor where it was dry and try to go back to sleep. The cleaning woman would come and pick me up and take me to the kitchen and take my wet clothes off and give me a coloring book, and she would say, "Come on, let's just go in here and color." A nun once gave me a Mickey Mouse watch that she had. They could be very kind.

You came back home full-time then after a few years? Was your mother really better by that time?

For one shining moment, there was a Camelot! She was a different person. By nature she was gentle and compassionate. I could make a real case for the positive value of lobotomies. I know hardly anybody thinks of it that way, but for me it was really true. I can honestly say I loved her a great deal. I can say that her lobotomy saved my life.

Was she able to stay out of the hospital for a long period of time then?

She did go back in a number of times because the madness would return. But she was out of the hospital a lot too. Once we were old enough, we stayed at home even when she was in the hospital. My older sister was like a mother, though, just like she had been all through the institution years. When my mother got discharged and would come home, there was always a lot of joy. It was kind of like the day would begin again.

She had been pretty depressed her whole life, I think, and she really wanted to try to be a good mother and she tried to do those things that mothers do. She could be grateful if you brought her a bunch of flowers. One of my absolute best memories of her is seeing her sitting in the sun reading a book. I remember just looking at her and thinking how gorgeous she was, just sitting there in the sun, reading a book.

That was when she was like my real mother. She could really laugh, not like a crazy person but just a normal laugh. She was kind and loving, and she could also call you on your shit; she would say to me sometimes when I was a teenager, "I don't know who you think you're talking to, but I'm not that person." She coped really well, and every day she told my father she loved him and every day he told her he loved her. There was just a very simple routine that my mother kept to, and it worked well. She could take care of my father, do laundry, cook a meal. Everything was routine and on a schedule. It was really okay.

Were you frightened of her then, when she was home? If you were hurt or scared of something, would she be a safe person to go to, would she comfort you?

She seemed well when she was home. If I fell down and got hurt, she would run to get me. I just remember her being loving and almost happy. I just realized lately that the lobotomies were a godsend to me; they gave me my mother back. I've been realizing that just very recently; that's why I keep saying it!

Were things about the same between her and your father, once she was home and well for longer periods of time?

He kept working as always, and he would come home and put all his money on the kitchen table, and then he would divide it all up and pay his bills $10 or $15 at a time. The most he ever made as a laborer was $21,000 a year. It took them 40 years to pay off a $13,000 mortgage on the house. On top of that he had to pay all of my mother's medical bills. At first she had gone to nice hospitals, private hospitals, but in the end it was state hospitals. Still, there were these huge bills, and it took him years to pay them off. I think my father was just happy to have her home, and he saw the financial burden as just part of what life dealt him.

You mentioned that your sister became a caretaker. Do you know what that was like for her?

From my point of view, I think I'm lucky that I had an older sister who was my surrogate mom. I've asked her how she was able to take care of all us kids when she was just a kid herself, and she said, "I didn't have any choice. I didn't even go to my senior prom because I had to take care of you guys."

I told her, "If I'm anything today it's because of you. How in the world did you do it?" She said, "Because every single day my father came home. And that's what saved *me*."

She adored him, and he loved her too. He saved her just by being the one coming home every day. He gave her hope. But she took on that burden, and I can see that she paid a price for it.

So there didn't seem to be any obvious negative feelings toward your mom, despite the violence and the years she was so sick?

I don't think anyone has ever spoken ill of her. My father never spoke ill of my mother—*never*—and only one time when he was much older did he say something that implied that her illness was hard on him, and he immediately apologized. He would always say, "She's a good kid."

* * *

How did you feel after the first interview?

I guess I could see that I'm actually a pretty resilient person. People have told me that, but I've brushed it off. But it doesn't mean I wasn't affected. I can see how I held onto the good moments that came at the bad times. It's kind of how I see the world, that something always comes along and helps me out of a dark place.

I was also thinking, what did I get from my mom? I got her depression, and I'm the only one of the kids that did inherit that. I also got her intelligence. Fortunately, I've finally found the right medication for the depression and it hasn't been a problem for five or six years now.

What happened as you got to be a teenager?

That's when the depression hit me, so I went through some pretty hard times, and I was pretty withdrawn. And then my sexual identity started to emerge. I went even deeper into depression and isolation, and it didn't help that I was going to one of the most violent high schools in the country. We lived in a section where the schools weren't great. We were pretty poor, the working poor; we had enough to eat but nothing extra. My father would never push for a promotion or take tests to upgrade his job; I think because of his ninth-grade education he was afraid he would look stupid. He was a very devout guy, but also very passive. So he never made much money, although he might have been able to do better.

Did you get any help for your depression? Was it recognized as a problem?

No, I thought the depression went along with being gay. I thought they were all the same thing. Being gay means having these kinds of depressed feelings all the time. That's just what it is. I've had this my whole life. As a kid I thought about just falling down the stairs, just letting it all go and falling down the stairs and it would be over.

What was it like at high school for you?

It was during the 1960s and 1970s, and the school was violent during the time the civil rights movement was going on. The streets could be violent; people could be screaming and alarms going off; it was really chaotic. That was hard for me to deal with—I just wanted to withdraw.

In high school, my brother was a kind of street guy. He got into drugs, and he really got himself into trouble. I was socially withdrawn and had very few friends. I did get into some acting and then was part of a theater company, and that was good for me.

What happened when you graduated from high school?

My parents didn't think I could go to college because we really had no money. But I applied for all kinds of scholarships and got into a small college in New York City, and I got noticed because it was very small. And a teacher spotted me and said, "What are you going to do when you get out of college?"—and I said, "I'm going to be an actor!" [Laughs] And he said, "Okay, come to this program at Harvard next week with me," and he introduced me to the whole world of communications. I had a knack for speaking in public, and I got comfortable being in front of groups. I don't know where that all came from, but it was just something I dove into. And that was the best for me! I've worked in that field on and off for years and used everything I learned from him.

Another person who came along at a tough time and helped you out?

I'm still in touch with him. He's the one who's my real father. He picked me up out of nowhere and asked me about what I wanted and what my plans were, and he introduced me to things that I was surprisingly good at. He even put me in front of our class to co-teach. And I wasn't the only one; he did this every single year with one student, and that was my year. He was really my mentor.

What happened when you were finishing up college—you were still living at home, right? How were things with your mother and father at that point?

I did live there, right. It was a very ritualized environment, almost military. Everything was in a specific location; the dinner menus were very routine, one day after the next. And she could cope; it did work.

Everything changed when I told them I was gay when I was in my early 20s. I had a girlfriend and my parents liked her, but I knew I couldn't really do that anymore. I told them one night, and the next morning my father came to my room at six in the morning and woke me up and said, "Give me your key. You have to leave, and don't tell anybody you're my son. I didn't make you to be like this."

Sounds like a total shock for you.

I remember walking around my room trying to figure out what to take with me. I wandered around in a daze and picked up different papers and books and stuff, and I ended up only taking this lamp my sister gave me. I didn't take a bunch of other stuff I should have taken—just this lamp! I have no idea what I was thinking. And it was snowing outside, and I'm getting ready to leave, and my mother comes up and says, "What's going on?" and I said, "He's asking me to go." And she didn't say anything. That was her chance, but she just didn't know what to say. It was horrible and unfair.

What did you do? Where did you go?

I did have a lover and I went to his place, but I know I stayed in that relationship too long because I didn't know where else to go. I would call home every few weeks, and they would just hang up when they heard who it was. No one would talk to me. I would write letters, and they would write "died" on the envelope and send it back. They didn't talk to me for 17 years and then finally relented. I still called occasionally, and finally one day my mother didn't hang up the phone. I was shocked! I said I was going to be in the area, and she asked my father and they said it was okay to come over, so I did. My mother gave me a big hug, but we never really talked about it.

So there was no explanation of what happened, or why they changed?

Not really. There were a few words with my father years later, but nothing at that time.

What were you doing during those years?

That's another story, those years. I moved to a couple of different parts of the country; I had a number of different jobs, and usually was in some kind of academic program. But depression was a real problem for me the whole time.

My siblings and I met up again when my mother died. They asked me to speak at her funeral and I thought, "How odd!" But I did, and they thought it was great, so that was when we started seeing each other again.

How was your mother doing after you reconnected with her?

Well, generally okay. We just never talked about their throwing me out. One thing stands out, though: she was doing pretty well, and I decided to ask her something. So I said, "Do you remember raising me?" She thought for a minute and then said very quietly, "No, I don't." I said, "Really?" She said, "No, I don't. Tell me, was I a good mother?"

And I said—I lied—I said, "You were a very good mother." She said, "Really?" And I said, "Yes."

And the truth is she was a good mother after her lobotomies. I could say that honestly—she was a good mother. But I lied about the years before that.

She was in her mid-70s when she started to go downhill, and during the last years she got much worse again like a lot of people who had lobotomies. That's what the research shows anyway. She had a lot of physical problems as well as the psychiatric problems and ended up in a nursing home. I could tell she was getting paranoid and delusional again. It was very sad.

How about you and your father? Did you ever talk about his throwing you out or anything about the 17 years?

At some point when my father got older, he did say to me, "I don't get this gay thing." I just thought, "Well, I don't know what to tell you. I have nothing to prove." My father died a few years later, and on his deathbed he said, "David, can you forgive me? There are two things that I can't forgive myself for and what I did to you is one of them."

And I said, "Well, we all make mistakes." But he was very Catholic and I knew it was important to him. And the truth was, he was trying to get to heaven, and I don't believe in heaven and I *didn't* forgive him for what he did to me. I could have told him the truth and let him have it, but I didn't have the courage or the desire to do to him what he did to me. He gave me life. I wouldn't be here if it weren't for him.

So I said, "I forgive you." And I lied. And it was a big load off my back. And he said, "Really?" and then he cried. I think I did the right thing, but I lied. I'm kind of glad I did, but I still struggle with it.

When you look back, how do you think your mother's illness affected you?

I was a very frightened child and I went jumping from one stone to another until I finally found a place where the stones came together. And when my mother had the lobotomies, then there was a place that was green and warm and had some people on it. The emotional impact? It makes me hypersensitive to people; it makes me wonder all the time: How do people communicate? How does a person become who they are? I've been in search of answers my whole life. What makes me me, and what makes you you?

What are strengths and weakness you get from this?

The lack of guidance early on really messed up my life, and I didn't get treatment and help early enough. Because there was so much just surviving we all had to do, there was nothing left over once the basics were covered. I lost a lot of years when I couldn't be very productive. I spent a lot of time pursuing degrees because I knew how to do that, but I couldn't maintain success in things because I couldn't build anything to the next level.

It took a long time to get on the right medication and the right dosage, but now I'm able to work and think and really do the kind of work I've always wanted to do and always felt I should be capable of. So now I'm working really well and can think clearly about the things that are important to me. I can do the abstract thinking that was so hard before. So I'm moving ahead and getting where I want to go. It's very, very satisfying. I've known forever that I have the potential; it's just taken a long time to get out of that fog.

How else did your family background, as well as your depression, affect your life, do you think?

My depression made me more dependent on my partners. I've had two serious relationships, both pretty long, with successful, well-educated men, but my depression skewed both of those relationships. I was too dependent, and I would get withdrawn and the depression would just take things over. I probably stayed in relationships longer than I should have.

How would you sum things up if that's possible? What's your reflection on where you've been and where you are now?

I feel like in the last few years, free of depression, I'm just starting out. I have my first apartment on my own; I have my mind; for the first time in my life I feel like I'm myself! I'm working my ass off but, hey, I'm working.

So I think, "How lucky can you get!?" How lucky can I get that my father wasn't an alcoholic, that he was just a simple man who knew a few words to say to me that gave me hope. How lucky can you get? How lucky can I get, that I found the right medication and it works and it's changed my life? Maybe it's strange, but that's how I feel.

ABOUT DAVID: MY REFLECTIONS

David's story is obviously complicated by a number of major events in addition to his mother's severe mental illness. His life is a series of dislocations and disconnections, yet his optimism seems to have remained intact.

David's older sister was a surrogate mother, and it seems she did a good job of caring for him in his formative years. It's significant that he didn't feel to blame for his mother's behavior and didn't feel it was up to him to make her better. When she finally came home from the hospital for longer stretches, and was even happy at times, David says in his characteristically buoyant way, "There was a Camelot!"

The remarkable thing is that there was no secrecy about her illness within the family, and even his teachers in school knew she was sick. However, the lack of accurate information in her own family created significant hardship; had his mother's extended family been more involved, the kids might have been spared living in an institution. David's grandmother was told by a psychiatrist that marriage would solve her daughter's problems, and when it didn't, she blamed the one person who loved and cared for her daughter with loyalty and devotion. It was a common belief in the 1940s that most of women's emotional problems could be "cured" by having a husband and children.

It's difficult to know what effect the "new" family life had on David as an adolescent, when his mother was well, as he became depressed and isolated for reasons related to his mood disorder and the emergence of his sexual identity. It's even more difficult to understand the aftereffects of his mother's illness because of two other major events: his coming out to his parents, and his abrupt eviction from the family. The family's rejection of him for such a long time—17 years—was a huge blow.

His recovery seems strongly related to finding a medication that truly helps his depression and makes him feel strong and independent for the first time in his life. His inborn nature is easier to discern now that his depression has lifted: he's an optimistic, sunny, energetic man whose motto these days is, "How lucky can I get!"

WHAT CAN WE LEARN FROM DAVID'S STORY?

Never underestimate the importance of inborn temperament! This is a man whose early trauma, subsequent isolation and seeming abandonment by his caretakers, and later expulsion from his family could easily have caused a life of bitter unhappiness. Add in the depression that plagued him for years, and we have a recipe for misery.

We can look for resilient features in his life, like the "nice woman with the long brown hair" who comforted him "when the music stopped." Nine out of 10 people living this story would barely remember the rescue and would be overwhelmed by the experience of loneliness and despair. One aspect of resilience is looking for, and remembering, the good moments despite the bad, and in David's story we can see that the moments of kindness and care were small events compared to the huge events they rode alongside like tugboats accompanying an ocean liner. To understand a child's ability to hold onto the reparative moments, we have to look at least in part to inborn temperament factors such as adaptability, curiosity, soothability, intelligence, humor, and a fundamentally sunny disposition.

Another crucial factor in David's resilience is the fact that he had a strong connection to his older sister. This kind of connection to just one significant person, when the parent cannot be that person, is a huge factor in mitigating the damage in a dysfunctional family. It also helped that there was no blame assigned and no expectation that the children would make their mother well.

3

Patrick: "Dad was like a dark shadow"

Patrick was raised in what he calls his "normal-looking" Irish Catholic family, with a loving mother, two brothers and a sister, and a father who was essentially absent. Though part of his story is that his father was diagnosed and treated as bipolar, there was much more beneath the surface. Patrick tried a religious life, but eventually became a school counselor and now works with adolescents. He's in his second marriage and feels he has been successful in "dodging the bullet" of his family legacy.

Can you tell me something about your early life?

We grew up in a place that was perfect for kids because there were so many places to explore and poke around. My father worked for the state and did well. The exterior of our family looked great, and of course being Irish that's what you look for, that the family always looks good on the outside. Mom stayed at home and started working part-time gradually. My dad was also president of the Lion's Club, and he was a volunteer fireman, and Mom was on the Board of Ed and did various other community things.

What do you remember about your father when you were young? Was there anything about how he acted that seemed unusual?

My dad seemed to become like a shadow as I grew up. I remember being a kid and his taking us to Keeney Park in Hartford and going sledding. But he was fading away. He wasn't quite there in the family, or if anything he always seemed to be irritated with us, with life, with everything.

I think it was when I was a young teenager that my mom told me he was manic-depressive, but I never saw anything that looked manic at all in any kind of way. But I certainly saw the depression, or rather, I felt it. So I grew up in a funny way kind of avoiding him but also always missing him. It's hard to say if anything seemed unusual; it's just the way things were. I did notice that he was really, really quiet and withdrawn. He also drank a fair amount—not to get drunk, I don't think, but he was just so withdrawn already that the drinking just made it worse.

I spent a huge amount of time outdoors. When I grew up your parents just said, "Go out and play, and don't come home till dinnertime," and that's what we did. I have a much better memory of playing ball, exploring the woods, just being outdoors playing than I do of being at home with my parents and siblings.

Dad worked all day in his regular job, but he also had a side job in a company that sold stuff like frat pins, sweatshirts, and that kind of thing. So he was out of the house most of the time.

Somewhere along the line my mom made it clear that she was staying in the marriage for us kids. I don't know if she said it outright, but it was crystal clear. Fat lot of good it did, because all four of us are in our second marriages. I can remember being resentful about it, but I wondered later if she really felt she had a viable choice. If she had left with us kids, the financial picture would have been pretty grim.

What was it like when your father was home, when there was a chance to interact?

Dinnertime could be torture between his being so silent and my mom catering to him. Also, my younger brother Mike was always more outspoken. I used to think of it as his putting his head up out of the foxhole. So Mike would say something provocative, and then Dad would be really critical and cutting. I would be thanking Mike for taking Dad's criticism because it meant I wouldn't get it. We all knew enough to keep our mouths shut, but Mike would talk back or speak up or say stuff that got him in trouble.

My dad wasn't abusive; there wasn't any hitting or anything. I never even saw him tee off on Mom emotionally. But he could be very critical and dismissive. I learned to be quiet and stay out of trouble, and unfortunately that made me into a junior conformist! Do whatever anybody else wants me to do instead of figuring out what I want to do, which has been one of my problems later in life.

How did your mother handle that, when your dad was sharp with you kids?

Sometimes she would counteract it right then, or sometimes later on she would say something to smooth things over. Over the years she would just say, "Don't tell your father, it'll upset him." But then we ended up with Mom and us over here on one side and Dad over on the other side. There wasn't a lot of overt hostility but a lot of resentment and tension and distance.

How did you actually feel about your dad?

I don't really know . . . he was just a mystery to me. [Long pause] That's so hard to answer.

Do you remember any times before age 12 or so when you and he had a good time, a good interaction?

I remember as a young kid he would take us to the park for sledding; I liked that. I think he played baseball with us a few times, but mostly my mom was the one who came to our sporting events. I don't remember any physical affection or any times he told us he loved us, anything like that.

What did you know about him and his own history?

He only said a couple of personal things. He told us once that when he was in college, he and some friends lived over a Chinese restaurant and they could smell the food cooking and he really liked that. I knew his father had deserted the family when he was 10, but he never talked about it. It's pretty sad I only knew a few things.

I did find out later that some of his family years ago had worked in the Danbury Hat Factory at the time when they used mercury to take the hair off the hide they used to make the hats.

So they could have become "mad as a hatter." Are you wondering if that would have affected them?

I wondered how many people it affected in my father's family and if that would account for some of the dysfunction. There was lots of alcoholism and depression in his family history.

What else do you know about your dad's diagnosis of manic-depression?

I don't know that much. My mom told me at one point that he was also suicidal, but I didn't see that. He was having a hard time at work when his boss was trying to give his job to one of his cronies, and I think that was really hard on him so he had electroshock treatment and landed at the Institute [a famous private psychiatric hospital in Hartford, Connecticut].

Who explained all this to you? Who tried to help you make sense of it?

I don't remember; but if my mom said anything, it would have been vague, like "he has stress at work" or something. I remember visiting him at the Institute and they explained something about putting electrodes on his head and that it would affect his memory.

What was it like to visit him there?

I was just stunned, to see him like that. He was just totally out of it. I think he had ECT [electroshock therapy] another time too, when I was 11.

He also had physical problems—he had a massive coronary when I was 21, and the prescription was bed rest, which is the worst thing. He seemed to recover, but then he had another heart attack at work and died soon after that.

How did you do as you went into adolescence?

I conquered all this by being a goody-two-shoes! I became an Eagle Scout, and my two brothers did also. When I was 16, though, I got this job with a guy who was a surveyor, and on Saturdays we would ride to work together. Erik was the most outgoing guy I've ever met. He was just really supportive and gregarious. He was such a contrast to my dad. Dad seemed to be irritated all the time, and Erik wasn't that way at all. He seemed to enjoy life, enjoy his job, enjoy my company—everything.

I was the dutiful son and Dad was the distant father. We both played our roles. He would be down on us about our grades, and the bad part was if he tried to help us with homework. He was good in math, but his helping was an ordeal. He was demanding and critical, and it was very unpleasant.

Did you feel you couldn't please him?

There was one time, even though he didn't say anything directly to me. When you became an Eagle Scout your parents are supposed to make some statement, and my father had written down something about how impressed he was when a tree came down on our property and "Patrick knew just what to do." I took this huge tree apart and knew all about how to do it. My mother showed me his letter after he died, and it was a revelation to me. I mostly remember just feeling a lot of resentment towards him.

Part of me was proud of him, his job and all that, because it was an important job and he got a lot of recognition for it. Most of the time he was just irritable or silent. He would get irritated if dinner wasn't exactly what he wanted or when he wanted it, and I don't think I ever saw affection between my parents.

Did you talk about any of this stuff with friends or your siblings?

Part of my problem was I never talked about any of this shit at all with anyone. I'm not sure I thought it was that unusual. But I sure wouldn't have told anyone my father was in a hospital. I don't remember talking with my sister or my brothers, either.

How did things develop for you after you graduated from high school?

I went to seminary, like a good Irish oldest son. I was there when my father had the second heart attack and died. I was 21 and he was only 53. And the night of the wake, my brother told me for the first time that my father had been having an affair. I was pretty naïve; I never suspected anything. But my brother was younger than me and he knew about it.

My brother told me he had followed Dad once. And my brother had this gun that was a family heirloom, from my father's father. So he had taken the gun with him and was looking for Dad, and had seen him being dropped off somewhere by his girlfriend. He told me the only reason he didn't kill my father was because he couldn't find any shells for the gun.

Finding out about my father having an affair, that was surprising. Maybe I had some inkling because it didn't seem totally out of the blue. But for me the biggest shocker was that my brother had this idea of shooting him because of it.

This was your brother who was so outspoken, right? Seems like he really felt things strongly for the whole family, including you. You were trying to stay under the radar, but he was expressing a lot of feeling about things that were really pretty troubling.

Sometime later Mom and I were going through the attic and looking for pictures, and my mom said, "I think you should see this," and there was a picture of my dad with this woman, at the Cape. Mom told me that she would get calls or letters sometimes from hotels saying, "Thank you Mr. and Mrs. O'Reilly for staying at our hotel," and of course she had never stayed at any hotel. So it was pretty hurtful.

What was your own reaction to it?

Of course I was pretty shocked and then angry with my father. And it seemed pretty black and white, even though I also realized that my mother had her own part in causing distance in their relationship. As we found out more information, it seemed like it wasn't just one short affair or even a few, but it was a 25-year relationship he had with this one other woman. When I talked about it with a therapist once, he said, "If that was a 25-year relationship, it must have been very important for your father." I'd never even thought of it from that vantage point, and it took a lot of the moralistic hot air out of my balloon and made it more complex for me.

Did you and your mother or siblings talk about it more, over time? Did you try to make sense of what had been happening over that whole 25 years? That's a pretty huge piece of information to try to put together with the way you saw your family up to that point.

I did talk with her when I was in grad school and we were supposed to get our family story. And when she was talking, at one point she mentioned his affair; then she got up from the kitchen table and went to the window and just stared out for a while. Then she said, "Despite all that, I really loved him." And I thought, "Geez, what do I know about what people go through and how they feel." It was a pretty telling moment.

What happened for you after your dad died and all this stuff came out about his affair and your brother's reaction?

I was pretty thrown by it all. I was thinking, "Here I am, son of a manic depressive and son of a womanizer; this is my destiny." I went into a pretty deep depression. When my dad died, it was a perfect storm. I had been unsure about my profession anyway, and I think I was heading for a depression anyway, maybe without even knowing why.

At the very beginning, when I first found out he had died, I felt a big relief actually. Our relationship had been so negative and so distant that I didn't feel a lot of sorrow right then. Then I went home and my brother told me about wanting to kill him because of the affair. That just floored me. Then soon after that the priests told me I had to take some time off before taking any vows because I just wasn't doing well. So I started seeing a therapist there, and it was really helpful to talk about everything and start understanding myself better. I felt very, very isolated, and in retrospect, I should have been on medication.

Were you concerned then about whether or not you were also manic-depressive?

Not really, I was just trying to survive. I was already depressed and then he died, and then the grief was loaded onto that. But it just seemed like a dark time for me, and I really needed help with it. I wasn't worrying about having his diagnosis. But I was like him in another way, in drinking too much, and it took somebody saying something about it for me to realize —hey, I've got to stop this.

It was a blow to be asked to leave seminary; and I was gone for a while, and in therapy, and it was a pretty long depression.

Did you tell anyone in your family you were going through this?

I wouldn't have said anything to Mom because she was always overly worried and anxious and I would have protected her. I probably didn't say anything to anyone else either; that's just the way the family is.

How did the rest of the family do after all this?

My sister had done really well, but she ended up marrying this handsome elegant guy who turned out to be a womanizer—how about that! She got divorced and remarried a really great guy. When he died suddenly, she was devastated. My brother the outspoken one wasn't a good student, and he always screwed around, but he joined the navy. Then he started drinking and drank himself out of the navy. My youngest brother seems to have done okay. I don't know how they handled all the family stuff emotionally because we didn't talk about it—again, classic for my family.

How did people around your father respond to him? What did they think about what was going on with him?

There wasn't much attention to him, really. There was other drama going on in my mom's family with my aunt and her abusive husband, and that was what people worried about and talked about. I know there were references to Dad's going out "bowling," and I started to think, well, was that when he saw his girlfriend?

I do think my mom was as depressed as my father was. Looking back, she must have been aware of the affair and must have been pretty unhappy about her situation. She was more focused on us and probably on her sisters with their marital problems, and not at all on herself.

So, in fact, your mother seemed to have known about your father's secret life for a long time and so she also had a secret life. So when he went "out bowling," she knew what was going on but didn't say anything. She really protected you kids from her own disappointments and anger and sadness about her marriage.

Oh, I remember one other thing my mother told me. Not long after they were married, my father was arrested in a local park for soliciting a pregnant woman. My mom knew somebody in the police force and they got it "taken care of"—but he could have gone to jail or lost his job. It certainly would have been extremely embarrassing. But my mom just had that Irish stoicism that women have, where she just trudged forward for the kids.

Neither family wanted my parents to get married, partly because they were young and partly because they were both helping support their own families. Mom was accepted at Connecticut College [this is a prestigious women's college in Connecticut], but she didn't go because her family needed her paycheck from work.

Your mother's story has been in the shadows here. She must have been a very good student with excellent potential to be accepted at a school like Connecticut College, and yet she had to give up that chance in order to help her family. Then she married a man who early on showed signs of not being able to be a good husband to her. Then the affair, which she knew about for years, must have been very painful for her as well.

She didn't complain; she would never have said anything about her own wishes or her own life. She was always there, but at the same time her life was always in the background.

What was her reaction to your father's death?

Well, I don't know. From her diaries I do know how unhappy she was, and I think it was in 1963 that the question of divorce came up, from her and also from him—and that would be shortly before he died. I know I had some relief when he died, and I would think she did too, at that time. Like she said later, she did love him, but I think if divorce had come up, she was pretty much at the end of her rope with him.

What did all this mean to you about how a boy grows up to be a man, and what kind of man he is supposed to be?

I was very anxious about being like him, for a long time. Am I going to be an alcoholic? Am I going to be a womanizer? I'm named after my father, grandfather, and great-grandfather, so that puts some pressure on too.

So how were you supposed to conduct yourself as a man out in the world?

I discounted the way he was a role model; I didn't want that, so I felt kind of lost. The guy Erik from that job I had in high school was the biggest alternative role model because he was so much different.

You had mentioned that you left the seminary and went to grad school?

Yeah, I didn't go back. I think I realized it wasn't right for me and they agreed. After I got over that depression, which lasted a long time, I got married to a depressed woman who ended up blaming me for her depression while I was trying to rescue her! We had two kids, which made it harder for me to get a divorce when they were youngsters. It was very hard to make that decision, but I didn't want to go down that road of having an affair, and I finally did decide. It was absolutely the right decision.

Your story almost suggests that your parents might have done better overall if they had gotten divorced, rather than stuck it out because of the kids.

I think I felt different after my divorce, like, "Now it's my life, the ghosts are gone, I'm not doing what my parents did." Despite the pain for my kids, I really didn't want to do what my parents had done. I've been very involved with my kids. I remarried, and with my wife now there's more equality and we're two independent people who are pursuing things on our own. She also does a lot of sports, the first woman jock I've ever known. And partly because of my father's bad health and heart attacks, I'm into fitness and nutrition and all that. When I was in my early 50s I had a mild heart problem, but unlike my father, within two hours of knowing I had a problem I was on the treadmill. No problems since then.

So in this marriage I don't have to rescue anybody, and I don't have to live in a state of tension and resentment. And we don't have to talk about everything because things just kind of go smoothly. It reminds me of a John Callahan cartoon with a picture of a woman and man and there's a big sign over the couch saying "Thank you for not talking about the relationship." I feel stronger emotionally than I used to, and more confident and more relaxed.

PATRICK'S STORY: MY REFLECTIONS

Patrick's story is largely a story of avoidance, denial, and forgetting—perhaps not uncommon for an Irish family in the 1950s. He mostly recalls the tension and discomfort of family times, as his father was alternately critical, biting, or silent. Patrick avoided any aggression, but it was there between his brother and father.

The disclosure of his father's 25-year affair has been hard for Patrick to integrate with the rest of the story, although if the affair were that long, it would have started before Patrick was even conceived! Adding this back into the family story, it suggests that his father was emotionally absent partly because he had another "family" or at least another wife, with whom he spent his time and presumably his emotional energy. Patrick's mother, knowing this was going on, had to be deeply disappointed, angry, and alienated from this nonresponsive man. Her connection would be to the children, and they certainly knew it but didn't know why.

Patrick's father's behavior seemed to him to indicate a quiet, unhappy, sometimes angry man, with a diagnosis of "manic depression" who sometimes was so depressed that he needed to be in a hospital and receive electroshock treatment. It's no wonder that there was little or no discussion about this, as it might have cast light on some of the underlying reasons he was so unhappy. The whole family, not just the father, was in essence living a double life.

I have to wonder if Patrick's deep depression, beginning possibly just before the time of the disclosure of his father's affair and persisting long after his father's death, may have reflected some of these heavy family secrets. The therapy he sought was certainly helpful in moving him out of this, and his divorce eventually broke what he feared was a family legacy of marital unhappiness. At present he's an energetic, healthy man who enjoys his life, his work, and his marriage.

WHAT CAN WE LEARN FROM PATRICK'S STORY?

This silence around his father's mental illness created a gaping hole in the middle of this family. The inner life of the mother remained mysterious, as she kept the family together and maintained good connections with her children.

Keeping the family together in this way was certainly beneficial, as Patrick is probably correct that life would have been a lot harder if his mother had asked for a divorce. But it did seem to require a certain amount of willful ignorance of the elephant in the room, and when families enact this kind of pretense, they often do repeat dysfunctional patterns.

One thing we learn from Patrick's story is that secrets often make relationships so thin they are almost transparent. His relationship with his father is like that: he knows one or two things about his father's inner life, and that's all. His father is a counter-role model, and there's no warmth or real connection, only Patrick's unfulfilled longing. Despite some closeness to his mother, he had no real idea of what her life was like, what choices she made, and why.

In this family it's likely that almost every secret kept by every family member was an attempt to protect other family members. However, the protection seems to have cost them any kind of genuine family warmth and connection.

4

Mark: "If you leave the house, you'll be murdered!"

Mark was encouraged to come in for the interview by his wife, who has been in therapy for some time. He was skeptical, never having talked to a professional about his family, but she thought that his background might have some bearing on things that hold him back now in adulthood. He works in the military, and he and his wife are hoping to start a family in the next few years. His mother was an extreme "worrier" about all kinds of things, and Mark describes the impact of his mother's anxieties and his father's disengagement on his growing up.

Can you tell me something about your growing up and what you think was different about your mom?

I remember more thinking that I was different, because the other kids in the neighborhood could do things that I wasn't allowed to do. Like they could go play basketball, hang around in the park, that kind of thing. I wasn't allowed to do that. I couldn't walk to the local store, and she didn't want me to walk down the street to the basketball courts. We grew up in a two-bedroom apartment in a suburb of Boston and I wanted to go outside with my friends.

There was a flight of stairs outside the apartment building and I was only allowed to go to the first step. She would say, "You're not allowed to go beyond the first step—it's dangerous. There might be somebody waiting to attack you—you could get killed doing that." There was just a lot of worrying all the time. My brother and I could go to this one small enclosed area to play that she could see from the window.

You have a younger brother, you said—was it the same with him, the same worry and anxiety?

It was just my brother and I, but I pushed things a little bit more than he did. I really didn't understand why I couldn't do things, because I was a good kid—I wasn't irresponsible at all. If I led the way, he might follow, but he wouldn't initiate pushing anything.

When you were a kid did you think she was right? It would be a natural reaction.

I don't recall that. I just didn't like the restrictions. We lived pretty close to our elementary school and she would walk us there. We couldn't walk by ourselves because somebody might kidnap us, we might get hit by a car, there might be drug dealers, everything. It wasn't a dangerous area at all, just a regular neighborhood. Other kids walked to school; other kids played outside.

I didn't have very many friends because I wasn't allowed to do very many things. My hair was even all shaggy when the other boys had short haircuts because she was afraid of me going to the barber. I didn't get it.

What was your dad's reaction to her restriction? Did he agree with her or did he ever step in to intervene on your behalf?

My father wouldn't get involved or interfere in her decisions, and I think part of the reason was because he was very concerned about money. So if she didn't want me to play football or basketball, then he didn't have to pay for the uniform or pay for any equipment. I really wanted to play hockey and football, and I would have been good—I'm very athletic—but she said, "Oh no, somebody will throw the ball to you and your spine will snap" or whatever, and my father was just as happy he didn't have to buy anything. I didn't get the idea that he agreed with her; it was just convenient for him.

What was your relationship like with him? Did he ever say anything about your mother's worries?

I don't think we've ever had a very good connection. He always wanted to do things on his own. My brother and I would get up on a Saturday morning, and Dad would've already gotten up early and gone to the beach by himself. He also kept food aside just for himself and never shared it. He was just extremely selfish like that.

He watched sports all the time on TV, but he never asked us to watch with him. We were just supposed to leave him alone. Once or twice I tried to sit down with him, but he didn't seem to like it. The main thing seemed to be he didn't want me to take any of his potato chips.

He was very tight with money, and my parents argued about it constantly. That's one of the main things I remember about him, just yelling and arguing about spending any money on anything.

Were there good times with your mother as well as these frustrating times where she was so restrictive?

Yeah. For example when I was young, she did have a job for a while so she had some of her own money. When she had a little of her own money, we would do stuff like go down to Mary's Pizza on a Friday night, and that was pretty exciting. It doesn't seem like much, but things were a little bit looser.

How did you feel towards her?

I always thought we were kind of close. She would talk to me about stuff sometimes, even though I didn't always understand. My mom would have these weird crushes on random men when I was growing up, and she would talk to me about how cute they were or how much cuter one was than the other. Not that she ever crossed any kind of line. Sometimes it seemed weird and I would say, "Mom, why are you telling me this?" Sometimes she would say this stuff in front of my dad. But it makes me think sometimes I don't really know my mom very well either. She used to tell me stories that I used to believe; like she told me one time Bob Dylan came to New York and she played the guitar for part of his opening act, that kind of thing. Afterwards I found out it was a whole big fabrication, like she was a big storyteller.

She told me her mom died really young and her father remarried. But the only person I ever met from her family was her aunt, who used to come visit. We liked her a lot; she would bring baskets of candy and presents with her and she was a lot of fun. I think she was kind of a substitute mother for my mom even though they also bickered a lot.

I never really got a straight answer out of my mother about whether she had brothers and sisters. I would ask her sometimes and she would just give me different answers at different times. Basically she would say, "Oh, they're all just horrible people." She also told me that she was homeless and lived in Chicago for a couple of years, but I don't know if that's true or not. She'll say sometimes she was a hippie in Chicago and she was homeless, and then once I joked with her about getting hold of her arrest record on the computer and she kind of freaked out.

So to tell you the truth, I really don't know her very well, or what she did growing up, any of that.

So obviously there wasn't any extended family on her side that you were involved with. How about on your father's side?

My father had some brothers, but everyone in his family seemed to be alcoholic and he didn't have a lot to do with them. Luckily, he never drank that I saw, so that was good.

What else stands out for you as a young child growing up?

Well, I knew from the time I was a kid that I wanted to be somehow in the military. I saw someone in a military uniform, and somehow I just knew that's what I wanted to do. And I told my mom, but of course she wouldn't want me to do anything like that. So she would try to convince me that the guy in the uniform was really a bus driver, because they wore uniforms. She kept telling me I really wanted to be a bus driver. She almost had me convinced of that when I was just a kid, but of course later on I knew the difference.

I think the thing that was the most frustrating was, I was really a good kid. I didn't do anything that should worry a parent. I didn't even go on my senior class trip because she said she would worry too much.

If I saw her with that worried look on her face, or crying, I would feel bad and guilty. But I would also think when I got older that I'm not doing anything wrong. I'm not causing a problem. But I would think of her sitting at home worrying or crying—that was hard.

Did you get angry as well as guilty?

I don't remember ever getting angry. I was just frustrated because there was nothing to make her feel better.

Were there other unusual things about your mother?

We hardly ever went out as a family, but this one time when I was a junior in high school, we went to some farm to pick pumpkins. Someone lifted up the corner of a tent and there was a barrel of pesticide. After that my parents went nuts with wanting to get organic food. They got hundreds of books about eating naturally and eating organic. In their house every single bookshelf is covered with books about vitamins and organic food. They started ordering vitamins online I think, and every square inch of the house is covered in vitamin bottles. That's been going on for years now.

What happened when you got into high school?

I didn't have a lot of friends, but the ones I had I wanted to have come over to my house sometimes. So I would clean the entire house by myself from top to bottom. And even before that, even when I was in elementary school and we lived in a different house, I would do the same thing. When

I was a kid things were pretty disorganized, but it wasn't a disaster. Once I got into junior high and we moved to this new house, every room was dirty and messy.

There was a lot more space than in the old house, and everything just kind of caved in. I used to go to my friend's house down the block, and I remember wishing that our house could look like their house. They had a living room that looked clean and I liked that. So I wanted to try to make our house look like that so my friend could come over and I wouldn't be so embarrassed. And at that time both my parents smoked all the time and it would get in my clothes, so when I went to school my friends would say I stunk like smoke. So at home the only place I had that would be safe was my own room. And I lined the door with some kind of cushioning so that the smoke wouldn't come into my room. I think that's when I started to say to myself, "I've got to get out of here!"

I would only let a couple of really good friends come over to visit and I would never say to them that I had to clean up the house. I would always act like it was just messy right now because my parents were doing something in the house, or there was some project going on; I would never let on that it was like this all the time. Because they would mess things up between the time I cleaned up and the time my friends actually came over. I would do everything in that house: I vacuumed from top to bottom, I did the hardwoods, I tried to organize things, I cleaned off the tables, everything.

But no matter how hard I ever cleaned, the house never really looked nice. The furniture was really old garbage furniture; they probably had it forever, and it was all shredded and scratched. It was really embarrassing. But my best friend would come over—she lived down the street—and her parents were about as weird as my parents were, so it was okay. My parents and her parents never met, but we talked about the weird things our parents did and we probably got to be closer and better friends partly because I didn't have to worry about her. I wouldn't be so embarrassed when she would come over.

How did your parents react to your doing this?

Sometimes they would throw me a bone and tell me how nice it looked; my dad might say something like, "The den looks good, you did a good job." But that would only last for maybe a day. And I remember that I would sweep up in the house and it would just be piles and piles of dirt, almost like you went outside and you were sweeping the ground. When I sweep up in my house now, there's hardly anything.

Did your mother embarrass you in public, say if she came to your school or anything like that?

She dressed in things that I would call kind of a throw-over, just loose things; she didn't wear a bra or anything. If she and my dad came to my school for some reason, they would dress up a little bit nicer, so I wasn't really too embarrassed.

How do you think this affected you emotionally in junior high school and high school?

I just mostly put my energy into trying to figure out how to get around things that bothered her. I'm almost more bothered by it now, looking back, in seeing how many opportunities other people had when they were younger. Then, it was just the way it was and I dealt with it. I didn't know any better.

Any other memories that are standing out as we're talking about this?

One really bizarre thing. I came home one night, and my dad, who was starting to get peculiar around this time, was sitting in the den naked, with some kind of plastic suit on, with a hat with some kind of tin foil antenna on it. He saw me, and he stood up and just ran downstairs to the basement. We never talked about it.

My friend Sarah, the one who lived down the block, she came in one time and saw my dad the same way. I asked my mom, "Why was Dad sitting in the living room naked with that plastic suit on?" And my mother just said, "Oh, I don't know what you're talking about." And he would disappear for the whole day when he wasn't at work and come home wearing jewelry or other things he had never had before. Since he's been like that, I don't really trust him to talk to him. He's always saying how he's sick and maybe he's going to die, but I really wonder about his crazy diet and all those vitamins.

Did you have any mentors or people who encouraged you? Teachers, coaches, people like that?

Not really, but I had an art teacher that I really liked, and when I graduated he sent me what was probably a generic letter that he sent to every student. But I still have it, and I laminated it. It said, "Live the life you imagine." I was in art club, and I took all my art classes from him, and we were on a first-name basis, but I knew it wasn't really personal to me—I realized it was generic. I guess I really did need to hear something like that from somebody I respected.

When it came time to go to college, I wasn't allowed to go away. And that's really all I wanted to do. So I went to a college nearby for two years and lived at home. But a friend at the time was going to a different college, and after my sophomore year I went to visit her there. I really loved the campus, and I loved the whole atmosphere, and I loved the whole idea of going away to school. And I thought, "There are places like this?" It was everything I wanted—the library, the river, my own room, and a salad bar in the cafeteria. So I transferred there and I never looked back.

But at home it was horrible. My mother was crying; she was totally upset. So it was really hard, but I wanted to do what I wanted to do. I transferred there and was there for the last two and a half years of college. It didn't cost any more money. The only thing that was disappointing was that because I went there so late, I couldn't really get on some of the sports teams, and it took time to make friends.

That took some determination, I can well imagine. What happened to your brother?

He stayed at home, and he and his girlfriend have a baby now although they're not married. They moved in together when he finally left home last year. We get along, but we're very different. He just doesn't have that much drive.

How did things change with your family when you left home and went away to this second college?

Well, my mother was very upset, and I did feel pretty guilty that what I was doing was making her feel so anxious and bad. I guess the thing that made me feel okay was that we talked on the phone every day. She would call me every day, and I got used to her being afraid of everything and it was okay to just talk to her most days. It can get a little annoying, but it's okay. I don't hold it against her.

* * *

It's been a couple of weeks since we last talked. Did you have thoughts or reactions afterwards?

I realized something that's probably a really obvious connection to what we were talking about. I was thinking, I haven't really traveled very much or gone to very many places; and I was wondering, why is that? It's because I'm worried that the plane is going to fall out of the sky. It's kind of obvious I guess, but I just realized after we talked that this is exactly what my mom would think or say, like, "If you go on a plane, the plane is in going to crash." I won't get on the plane because I'm afraid of dying on the plane.

I was talking to my wife the next day, and I told her about it. And I had to laugh—this is just so obvious! It really opened my eyes because I always have to drive places, so we can't travel all that far.

So I have some time off in a few weeks, and I said to my wife, "Let's go somewhere!" She said, "Okay, where do you want to go?" Well, I always wanted to see the Grand Canyon so I said, "Let's go there." So I booked it! And we're leaving in a couple of weeks. We're going to stay for a week and see a lot of different places. Then when we get back I want to plan a trip to the Hoover Dam. Then I want to go to Europe, I want to visit every state, and I want to go to Iceland.

I'm impressed! Sometimes those "obvious" connections are the hardest ones to see. That's impressive that even though it's making you a little anxious, you're going to push through the anxiety and do something you've always wanted to do.

It's not like it's the most comfortable thing in the world, but I'm going to do it.

Let's go back to where we ended up last time, with you finishing up college. What happened after that?

My mom wanted me to come back home, but I found a job an hour away with room and board so I just kept going. It was a no-brainer. Then I started getting involved with the military and that's been great for me. She's finally okay with that.

How does your wife get along with your family? Did you have to explain about your mother to her?

My wife actually gets along pretty well with my mother and talks with her. And in fact, my mother actually left the house and came to our wedding. That may have been the last time she left the house. My mom's main form of communication is her iPhone, and she and my wife talk on the phone or e-mail each other a lot. I kind of like it because it deflects my mother's attention away from me.

Apart from the travel phobia, which you seem on your way to conquering, how else do you think your family has affected you?

I've been thinking about that. I recently turned down a possible promotion in my job. It would have meant that I would've gotten assigned another military training, then I would've been assigned a location and my wife and I would've had to move there. But they don't tell you where you're going beforehand. So I didn't know where we would be. I just had too many anxieties about it. What if I had to travel and fly? What if I didn't like it? I did all the work to get that promotion possibility, but I couldn't do it. So I think that's one place that I've really been affected.

I think it's been just recently I realized I can buy something if I want to. If I want new sneakers, I can go get them. We both work and we save a lot. I don't want to be like my dad, and if I hear myself sounding like that, I told my wife, tell me and I'll stop. And I don't want to be selfish like him.

How do you feel about your parents now? How are they doing?

My feelings about my mom haven't changed much over time, but my feelings about my dad have. I don't think we ever had a good relationship, and I have a hard time not thinking of how little he had to do with us as kids and how off to himself he's always been. He's just never been that involved. He had some chances to do more with us, and he just never did. It's hard to think that he really cares all that much.

I'm worried about my mom's health. She says she has rheumatoid arthritis and then she'll say she has fibromyalgia. So I don't know; she's probably told me a dozen different diagnoses over the years. But she hasn't left the house for a few years now and it's not a healthy place to live. They hoard vitamins and books, and when you go over there every single place is just crammed with vitamin bottles and all that stuff. And they still smoke if that makes any sense at all.

They actually get along better now. But he still thinks he's going to die, and when I'm on the phone with her I hear him yelling in the background, "Tell him I'm dying!" and she just says, "Oh, be quiet, you're not dying." But they seem friendlier with each other than they used to be and they don't argue much anymore.

Do you think about having kids, having your own family? Any concerns about passing any of this on?

Yeah, we want to have kids. I haven't worried about passing anything on, but I still want to wait a while because I feel I have so much catching up to do. I want to be free, I want to travel, and I want to do all the things I want to do. Because when I have kids I want to pay attention to them, do things with them. And share my potato chips with them!

ABOUT MARK: MY REFLECTIONS

Mark's story is a mixed one. His mother's dysfunction is obvious, although we have no idea of its origins. Her very excessive fears and anxieties definitely had a negative effect on Mark's ability to move freely into the world and made him more fearful of some things he didn't even notice until after his first interview. Her other oddities are equally problematic:

her fear of leaving the house, and the possible hoarding problem, which may be getting worse.

It's difficult to tell how much impact her physical limitations have had on her. Any of the diagnoses he mentions could seriously limit her mobility and ability to function. It's likely that the physical and mental are folded together in a way that would be impossible to sort out: since she's already anxious about dangers outside her home, physical problems would make it more legitimate to stay in. And if she's physically limited, her anxiety about going out would only intensify over time.

Her family background and personal history are equally mysterious. It's certainly quite unusual that she hasn't even told her children how many brothers and sisters she has and what happened to her parents. No doubt these would cast some light on her present state, but Mark may never know more than he does now. On his father's side, there's been little family contact there either. So this family has been isolated from any extended family and from most other social contacts, and seems to exist in its own little bubble.

On a more positive note, Mark's mother seems in many ways to have been a good, kind, loving presence and seems to have given Mark a solid foundation. He loves his mother even as he evades her neediness and her worries, and he wants to help her and to improve their relationship. He reserves most of his negative feelings for his father, who seems to have ignored his sons and lived an almost solitary life in the midst of the family. Mark feels much more put out by his father's self-centeredness and isolation than he does by his mother's extreme ideas, isolation, and anxieties. He sees his mother as controlled by her fears, while his father seems to have more options but exercises them selfishly. His father's strange behavior is also off-putting to Mark, and his mother's collusion with it leaves him in the dark.

Mark did well to take advantage of the freedoms offered to him by his art teacher and by the friend he visited in college. His readiness to be free of his limitation also showed itself in the speed of his booking that flight to the Grand Canyon. It deepened my conviction that sometimes just telling your story is enough to get things moving in a good direction.

WHAT CAN WE LEARN FROM MARK?

His story reinforces the idea that some closeness and goodness in a relationship can mitigate against other damaging aspects of that same relationship. His mother was loving and attentive, but he would have been better off if there had been help along the way.

We also see a lot of resilience in Mark. Instead of spending his energy on trying to change his parents, he simply "did it himself," especially as an adolescent. I think coping strategies that take children further away from dysfunctional parents may be better than strategies that lock them into trying to change/help/rescue those parents. He did try to help but had a realistic sense that he wasn't doing anything wrong to make his mother worry. He was able to follow his own path, but in the process he didn't reject his mother. She, in turn, was neither blaming nor punitive.

Mark doesn't seem to have the survival guilt some men experienced, and he feels entitled to pursue his own life even though he wasn't able to rescue his mother and make her feel more comfortable. He's able to express affection for his mother as well as guilt and remorse that sometimes his actions cause her to worry. Because he's more conscious of his positive feelings, he doesn't seem to feel guilty if his life is more satisfying than hers. When people can accept both positive and negative feelings toward their parents, they are less likely to be driven by unconscious guilt that often finds expression in self-sabotage.

5

Ben: "Our family code: Protect Dad at all costs"

Ben grew up in New York State with his parents, his older sister, and two younger sisters. His father was a remarkable artist and often a wonderful teacher of things that interested him, yet he could also be erratic and self-absorbed. He was also psychotic and delusional at times, and he was hospitalized several times with a diagnosis of bipolar disorder, spending a total of three or four years in various hospitals. Ben has struggled to integrate the good and bad aspects of his father, wanting to be a loyal son yet needing to face the ways in which his father failed him. Ben and his wife have dealt courageously with their son who has also been diagnosed as bipolar, and Ben is determined not to continue the family legacy of silence and stoicism.

What's the first time you realized there was something wrong with your father?

The first time was when I was about six, and my parents were planning a trip to Jamaica. Then suddenly my dad had to go to the hospital, to the VA, and I think he had a lot of electric shock therapy. My image later was that it was kind of like *One Flew Over the Cuckoo's Nest*. When he came home he had these boxes with each compartment labeled with what pills he had to take and when to take them. My sisters and I would help him put the pills in the boxes every weekend. He never discussed with us what the pills were for; we just helped him put them in the boxes.

It was a long time before I made the connection between the pills and the trips to the hospital.

What was your dad like before that happened?

He was very playful. I remember him doing hand puppet shows with elaborately built hand puppets. He would hang a sheet between the living room and the kitchen, and then we would do these amazing shadow puppet shows. He would practice his art history lectures on the family, and I always loved it when he would come home with a movie projector and cans of film, and we would watch movies from his university library.

I remember a lot of good things about his being very kind and very relaxed about a lot of things. When I was a kid I would go to my father's studio and he would let me do whatever I wanted—make dinosaurs or make buildings or I could also look at the nude models who were there for classes. There was just no big deal about my hanging around and doing whatever. If the cleaning man was around, my father would talk to him with the same amount of respect he would show the dean if the dean happened to come by.

As wonderful as all that was, my main connection to him was through what *he* wanted to do. For example, when I was in a play he would go to the play. When I sang in the chorus, he would go to hear the performance. He never once went to a soccer game or a swim meet or a track meet because he wasn't interested in it. It would never occur to him to go just because I was in it or that I might like to have him there. When there was a confluence of what we were interested in, it was wonderful. He was warm and he was a wonderful teacher. He was very loving and affectionate.

Yet there were also times when he had no judgment at all. He had been in WWII and that was very traumatic for him. One of his comrades was killed while saving my father's life. I heard a lot of pretty horrific stories when I was very young. He was also involved in liberating one of the concentration camps, which was traumatic for him. Most of the soldiers who liberated the camps took a lot of pictures and when I was seven, he decided that would be a good time to show me his pictures. To this day, I wish he hadn't done that. You can't deal with it when you're seven years old, but he didn't think of that.

When he went to the hospital, did anyone talk to you about that? Did your mother say anything to you? How was it handled?

No, we didn't talk about it. It was just very matter of fact and everything went on as usual. I wondered about it, but the message was very clear: you just didn't ask questions or discuss it at all. My mother made everything "normal" and that's how you were supposed to respond.

Are there other memories that stand out from those early years?

There's one funny one, when I was about nine. I overheard him telling my mom he had invited an Indian woman to dinner. I decided to get a Mohawk haircut to impress her, so I asked my dad to give me a Mohawk and he just agreed with no hesitation. I guess it just seemed like an offbeat creative thing to him. Later on I saw his car drive up and this woman in a sari got out of the passenger side. I was so embarrassed! There was a later time when I was a teenager and had kind of long hair, and the assistant principal called my father into a meeting so he could tell him to have my hair cut. My father came in for the meeting, and his hair was longer than mine. That was the end of that meeting.

Was there a downside to his being like that?

Yeah, in a lot of ways he was like an adolescent. He didn't have any better judgment than an adolescent. Even though he could also prepare a very detailed art history lecture, with 150 slides, and a totally organized presentation, when it came time to do other things, you never knew what he was going to come up with. So he was fun in a way, and creative and offbeat, but as far as being a reliable adult, he really wasn't.

When did you start thinking of your family as being different?

I always knew my dad was different. He wore different clothes, he sometimes wore a beret, and sometimes he would wear some kind of scarf around his neck and I found that embarrassing. He could also do things that the other dads couldn't do because he was more creative. The other dads I knew had what I considered very boring jobs. They went somewhere during the day and did something and then came home. My dad's work was visible and interesting because he had a studio in the house.

Occasionally, other kids would come over to the house and they didn't seem to think anything bad about him. Sometimes he would teach them things. He would help me with school projects sometimes.

Your family spent some time in Europe when you were growing up, isn't that right?

Yes. My father planned this grand trip to Europe when I was about 10. The whole family would go and see all the art museums, and visit different countries. It was very exciting and we were going to stay for several months.

We had been in Italy for about three months when my father got very ill. He had to go to the hospital, and I remember my older sister and me being

taken to see where he was. It was like a big old prison with these huge for-
bidding walls and iron bars and we could see him through the iron bars of
the gate. Thank goodness we didn't go in; it would have been too frightening for me.

I don't know how long he was there, but during all that time my mom
made everything seem very normal. She didn't speak any Italian, and she
had not been the one to plan the trip, and here we were in Europe with my
father in the hospital and she had to manage four kids. I don't really know
how she pulled that off without showing any particular stress.

*Do you have any recollection of what led up to his needing to be
hospitalized?*

I remember asking my older sister what was going on, but she wasn't
that much older than I was and she was clueless too. I wondered why
my daddy was sick and why he was in that place, and when would we
see him again. And I remember it really didn't seem like a hospital—it
seemed like a prison. I was confused about that. My mother went to visit
him, I remember, because my older sister and I had to watch the younger
kids when she was there.

Before he got sick, I spent a lot of time with my dad in the studio he had
in Rome. When he was okay, it was great to be with him. He taught me
everything—how to use plaster, how to carve, how to draw, how to paint,
how to sharpen chisels—just anything and everything.

But there were other times that were scary. He really went mad one day
in the studio in Rome when he was working on a set of sculptures he
called "The Harpies." I swear that there were times in the studio with
the way he acted, I could tell that he was actually seeing these things,
these images. He really saw the demons coming down. I knew something
was going on, because he would suddenly start acting very frightened and
he would cover his eyes and moan.

Other times we would go out and he would take his sketchpad, but suddenly he would get frightened of something and we would have to go back
right away. Once or twice he talked about "the harpies" and what he saw.
It was frightening, but I didn't have any place to turn. I couldn't talk to
anybody about it. It was not something my mom would ever ask about,
and I thought it was just something between Dad and me.

*When did you notice that this was different from the way other kids related
to their fathers?*

It wasn't until college, really. I didn't have much of a peer group.
If I hung around with people, it would be my dad's students or other

people like that. My father didn't set a great example there; he was very sensitive to imagined slights, and he would have friends and then get upset with them for some reason and not see them anymore. I didn't feel I had a lot in common with kids my age and I was more likely to do my own thing.

Were there other adults in your life who were important to you?

I ran track for a while and played soccer, but it was always hard. My track coach was tremendously helpful to me. Once he told me, "Look, Ben, you don't have what it takes to be a track star. But what you do have is the best attitude of anyone on the team, and you work hard and put in 110 percent. So when you find out what your passion is, you have what it takes to be a star doing that." And that meant more to me than what any other teacher had ever said to me. I wish my dad had said that.

Was there much extended family on either side? Were they involved in your family as you were growing up?

My grandparents died early, and my mom had some siblings she didn't get along well with. I had an uncle and aunt on my dad's side and I liked them, but we didn't see them very often. Some of my dad's family was killed in the Holocaust. I know my parents had friends, but my dad also was alienated from a lot of them. We ran into a guy just casually once when we were out, and it turned out he was my father's best man at his wedding. I couldn't fathom how you could lose track of people like that.

How did your mother cope with all this? What was she like?

My mom seemed resigned to the role of being my father's caretaker. She was an incredibly bright woman who never went to college until we got back from Europe. When she was younger she had been a coloratura soprano and had sung in the New York opera company. She gave all that up when she met my father. She also developed some heart problems during the time I was growing up and had some big surgeries when I was in college. She became very weak and didn't have much stamina. By the time I was a senior in high school, she was having trouble walking across the room without getting out of breath.

How did you see your parents getting along with each other?

My father said to me more than once, "Your mother is my ambassador to the world. I just don't understand people and I don't understand what they mean and what they need." My parents had some problems later on, but at that time we all followed that "omerta"—the Mafia word for "code of silence." It was "Protect Dad at All Costs." No matter what he did, she would make it work out okay.

He could also be very impetuous and unreliable. The whole family could be ready to go out somewhere, with their coats on, and he might say, "Oh, I have to go to my studio and do something," and we would be standing there for half an hour or an hour until he reappeared. Once we went down to his studio after a long time of waiting for him, and he had fallen asleep there.

How did your mom handle that kind of thing?

Like a saint! Very occasionally she would get pissed at him and say something like, "Do you have to do that right now?"

Were you afraid of having the same kinds of problems that he had?

There were times in my teens and 20s when I wondered when I would go mad like my father. There were times when I felt I was right on that edge of the abyss and I could feel the breezes, and I could feel the power of something sucking me over the edge. I stood fast and didn't go over, but I really felt it, being on that edge.

Was there anyone you could talk to about that?

No, I was pretty solitary back then. I studied alone and I worked alone. My dad wasn't a good role model for how to make friends, and he didn't help me with the usual father-son things like how to talk to girls or ask a girl out on a date. He told me that my mom was the one who knew how to do social things, like remembering people's birthdays or being sociable at a gathering. He didn't know how to do those things.

He was also the kind of person who would carry around, metaphorically, a pocket full of stones. Each stone was a very precise memory of some wrong that had been done to him, real or imagined. When he talked about people he would talk about these slights, not the good things. I've always known I don't want to be like that. I want to focus on the good things about people. But he wasn't the right person to teach me.

Were there problems when you went off to college?

No, I knew what I was interested in and where I wanted to go. And there wasn't a lot going on with my dad at that time, as far as I knew. But right after college there were a couple of strange things. First, I went to visit him when he was in California doing some teaching. He suggested we go to Disneyland, and when we were there we almost immediately ran into this woman Rose. They had been in love before the war and then broken up; then they both had married other people, and she was a widow at the time we "ran into" her. It took me 20 years to realize—"Hey, that wasn't a coincidence!"

Then another shocker. He was helping me move my stuff to a new town and we took his car, and there was a grad student traveling with us. We stopped along the way and got a motel for the night. By the way, I've never told this story to anybody. Late at night this woman came to my room and wanted to have sex with me. It was so bizarre. I pretty much fended her off because I was practically engaged to someone at that point. The next morning my father was miffed with me because he had expected that she would spend the night with *him*. I was like, "Holy fuck. What is this all about?" Here I was thinking that she was his graduate student, and then she came on to me, which seemed very weird. Then it turns out that he's expecting to have sex with her and he's mad at *me*!

I started to put things together and I realized he had probably had some affairs with graduate students for a long time. My mother found out about one of them and it broke her heart, but she stayed with him. I was in college when I found out because he actually told me himself. He told me that he had talked to my mom about it and she had given her blessing for him to fool around. I didn't know what to think—this went way beyond having bad social skills, to think for one minute my mom would have given her blessing for his fooling around? She had gone ballistic when she found out.

My feeling was he had betrayed my mom and that he was really stupid and adolescent about it, and a piece of his madness came through because he just did not get it. I don't know if he was stuck somewhere in an adolescent mind-set, or if he had a personality disorder, which he probably did on top of the bipolar.

You said they stayed together even after she found out about at least one affair. Was she still acting as his ambassador to the world? How was he functioning in general during this time?

He had a university position at that time, and the other professors who worked with him were tolerant of his oddities because he was such an incredible sculptor and such a good teacher. But he himself knew that without my mother, and without these men in the university who protected him, he probably would have ended up homeless, or locked up in a mental institution or killing himself.

How were you getting along with him during that time, after college?

I had gotten into medical school, which was my dream. And when I told him he said, "This is the saddest day of my life." I asked him what he meant by that, and he said, "It means you're going to lose your art." That was devastating to me. I ended up leaving medical school after a couple of years and going into visual arts, and I really am wondering now, as we're talking, whether or not I would have done that if he hadn't said what he said. It was years before he recognized the legitimacy of what I do, and it was probably a lot of years too late to really support me.

How were you doing in your personal life during that time?

I had met the woman who's my wife, Megan, and she was trying to figure out this family of mine. We started off on our own lives and had to make some boundaries for ourselves, and that's a whole other story. She's been really helpful to me in understanding some of the family dynamics, and she said to let you know that she'd be glad to come in and talk with you as part of my interviews.

I'd love to get her perspective, and it would give your story another dimension. Let's include her next time. What were the things you were struggling with, with your dad, over those next years as you were raising your own family and working out your own career?

We lived several hours away from my parents so there was some distance. But my father did do some strange things. He would just show up sometimes, in his red pickup truck. Once we saw his truck in the driveway, but he wasn't there. He showed up a few hours later with his accordion because he had been over to a golf course serenading the golfers and was surprised the clubhouse hadn't invited him in for a drink to thank him for playing his music. He just had no clue.

Another time he and I went to the bookstore downtown, and I was in a separate aisle and he started yelling, "Where are you? Why have you left me stranded here?" So he would just get crazy sometimes.

Were you in doubt about becoming a father yourself?

Absolutely not. I wanted to be a father forever, probably since I was 10 years old. I always wanted that and knew it. And even though I couldn't have put it into words exactly, I knew I didn't want to be the way my father was with me.

Did he have much to do with your two sons? How did you explain him to them?

Because of the distance, there were just some visits and they seemed to go fine. The boys were young and we didn't really talk about him to them. But despite the things that I did right with my sons, my father's madness skipped a generation and brushed by me, but it hit one of my sons full in the face. I felt guilty about it for a long time, and against all logic I still feel guilty sometimes. Our oldest son has had problems since before college, and my response is to be there for him without judgment anytime he needs me.

That must have been tough to handle and I'll want to hear more about it a little later on. If we can go back to your dad for right now, what are your thoughts about how to understand all the different aspects of his personality?

The good stuff about my dad was so incredibly good, and then the crazy stuff so incredibly crazy, it's hard to hold in my head at the same time. And it's been hard that my wife never saw the good side of him, only the bad. The good parts represent the soul of the man, and the bad parts are the things he couldn't control. Why should I honor anything that probably tortured him as well as hurt other people?

That may make it hard to be able to understand him as a whole and very complex person.

I really hate to use the word "gypped," but I'm just recently realizing how deprived I was of a normal father. He couldn't give me the regular normal things fathers can give sons. There was no one to talk to about it. There was never any place where it was safe for me to talk about it.

He's an unusually complex person to try to understand. How old were you when you started talking to people about him?

Oh, I never talk to people about the difficult parts. Just about what a great artist and sculptor he was. I don't talk about this other stuff. I saw a therapist once, but he ended up falling asleep and that was the end of that!

Were you ever able to talk about him with your mom?

No, she died very suddenly when I was in my 40s, and we were still in the "Protect Dad at all costs" mode. So we never were able to talk. Whatever her burdens were, she took everything to the grave.

What would have helped, if something could have been changed?

It would have made a difference if Mom had talked to me about what was going on. If I had known what was wrong with him and how to understand it. I have a vague memory of her saying something like, "He means well" and I should forgive him. That's the closest we came to a conversation. Once I was out and on my own, we always talked on the phone a few times a week, but that topic was always off limits.

* * *

It's been a few weeks since we last met. Did you have any thoughts about our last interview?

Yes, it gave me a lot to think about. And it took more out of me emotionally than I thought it would, but I think that's been good.

I realized that I've brought the "Protect Dad at all costs" habit into work. I should have stood up to my last business partner a lot sooner than I did. And my current partner is an older, very powerful man, and I've known I have to be more assertive with him. But I think after our talk I've been a little more confident in telling him that what I want and need is as important as what he wants and needs. He's fine with that, but it doesn't come naturally to me to see it that way.

The other question that's glaringly obvious is how do I put my father in perspective without making him a villain? I want to honor my dad's struggle and also acknowledge that it damaged me.

My bias is obvious—therapy can be really helpful with that kind of thing.
Maybe it's time to find a therapist who doesn't fall asleep!

Definitely! We were going to talk about your son today, and then also meet with Megan and get her perspective. Can you tell me a little of what happened with Elias?

We started to realize something wasn't right with Elias when he was about 15. He could behave normally in every way, or so it seemed, but he was really having an awful time. He was in a high-pressure school, but he had insisted that he wanted to apply there and we didn't stop him. When he went to college, he really couldn't manage it and had to withdraw. He got suicidal and had to be hospitalized and that was extremely hard for all of us. Megan and I were blindsided because he had covered so well.

Since then he's been back to college then had to withdraw again, and he's been hospitalized several times. There have been times he and I have holed up in a motel near his school, working like mad to finish his papers so he wouldn't flunk out. That was probably necessary and helpful a couple of times, but that's not where we are now.

What's it been like for you to have your son be so troubled?

I decided that I don't bear the responsibility for genetics, but I do bear the responsibility for how I deal with what's happened. So I recognize it and help him as best as I can. There's that irrational feeling that I'm his parent and he got this because of me, but I have to do something productive and not be stuck there. There are kids who have cancer and have a much more difficult situation than Elias's. Relatively speaking, he's lucky. Bipolar disorder is treatable, more so than a lot of other genetic disorders.

How much does he know about his grandfather's illness?

We hadn't told the kids a lot when they were younger, but as this developed we did talk to him about my dad. He was kind of freaked out at first, but now we're more focused on how to go forward. His experience definitely doesn't have to be a repeat of my father.

How are you doing it differently?

First, I'm committed to being there in whatever way Elias needs me to be. I've been the one to go with him to the hospital; I've been the one to drop work and respond when there's been an emergency. That feels very important to me. I'm not going to make it a big secret, and we do talk about it. Megan and I talk, and people that we're close to know about it. And our younger son knows what's going on.

Has it been hard to not let guilt push you into rescuing him more than is good for him?

I think for a few years it was important that I did lean over backwards to do anything to help him. We considered having him come home, but he wanted to stay where he was in school. So last year we found an excellent treatment center there and we got him connected. He was going regularly and really liked it, and they really understood him and we were impressed that they really knew what they were doing. So he went for a while, and then he stopped going and he didn't tell us.

So Megan and I talked about it, and we realized that he has to do his part. We can't do his treatment for him. He is capable of managing his own therapy and his own illness. And I confronted him. I said, "Right now, we're paying your way on absolutely everything: your apartment, your car, everything. We've given you a very expensive opportunity to get better and to have the best treatment. If you don't want to do that, then you're on your own financially from here on out."

I can't tell you how hard it was to have that conversation with him! I think we were just holding our breath. It's very scary to say this to a child who has been suicidal at times. But it worked. He stepped up and he's now doing much better. He's working, he's saving money, and he went back to the treatment center and he's still working with them.

That was an impressive thing to be able to do, given your history.

I think so too. But it seemed like the only way to do it. Now, he calls home to say hi and we have great conversations. We're all starting to feel like maybe we've come through the worst of this. Maybe it can just be a manageable chronic illness that he has to take care of. He's 25 and has his whole life ahead of him.

How are you doing with your younger son?

We've been open with Aaron without making it the main event. He and his brother have their ups and downs like any brothers. It's just part of the family conversation.

* * *

Megan is joining us to talk about her perspective on coming into Ben's family, and about how she and Ben have responded to their son Elias's illness. Megan, tell me what it was like when you were introduced to Ben's family.

Megan: All I heard about Ben's father, Nathan, was how wonderful and smart and talented he was. And he was all of those things, of course. So I came into the family with no forewarning and no awareness.

Probably one of the earliest times I got a sense of how the family was, was when we went to Ben's parents' house for a few days over Thanksgiving. That was all okay, but then on Thanksgiving Day itself, we were supposed to all go to dinner at Ben's sister's house, about 20 minutes away.

We had talked about what time we would leave, and we got our food together and all packed up. We were just about to go and Nathan suddenly got up and said, "I have to go work on my sculpture," and he went off to his studio. So I thought, "Well, I guess he'll join us later." Then everybody took off their coats and sat down. I was just dumbfounded. I'm looking around thinking to myself, "Are you kidding me?" So I said, "Joanie's expecting us in a little while," and somebody said, "He has to do his work," like they just had to explain this obvious thing to an ignorant outsider.

Well, I'm a pretty direct person. I'm from the Midwest. So I said, "Well, let's just go ahead. He has his car and he can join us later on." Ben's sister said, "We can't do that!" And I just said, "Why not?" and that seemed to unsettle things. I wasn't trying to upset anyone and I didn't say it in a challenging way. I was just really asking—why can't we go and he can come later? Is there some reason that's not the solution here? So I started to go and they finally all got up and put their coats back on and off we went. And Nathan wasn't too happy about it later on because that had never happened, evidently!

What was your take on that, Ben?

Ben: I never even noticed that we did that! It was just the way it was. I started to see things a little differently after that. Megan wasn't welcomed with open arms, because she's not Jewish and she had been divorced and—worst of all—she was a mental health professional! My

mother definitely didn't like that, because I think she'd had it with therapists by that point.

Megan: She didn't warm up to me until we had kids, then she was fine.
I always got along with Ben's sisters and the other relatives, but Nathan
and I never really warmed up to each other.

The other thing that was difficult was when Ben's parents would come
to visit; they would sometimes show up unexpectedly, and when they
did Nathan was supposed to be waited on hand and foot, by me, no questions asked. His mother would be incensed that I didn't jump out of bed
first thing in the morning to make Nathan's breakfast. The first time it happened was right after our honeymoon and we were exhausted. That didn't
go over well, I can tell you!

Ben: I would try to manage my dad, but he was a one-man herd of cats.
The thing that's been hardest for us is that Megan never ever saw my
father's good side for herself. She knew my stories about how wonderful
he could be, but he was never that way around her and she never saw
him in that light. So her take on him has always been more negative and
then I'm in the position of always defending him.

Megan: I know it's been hard. I realized early on that this was Ben's
father, and I would tone it down. It just put Ben in too much of a bind.
But there was one time early on when Ben took a stand and I think that
was really important.

I remember this like it was yesterday! I had just given birth to Elias who
came early, and it was a very difficult labor and delivery. And we had the
pediatrician do the circumcision in the hospital before I brought him home.
I had just gotten home and there in the pile of mail was this three-page letter,
this diatribe, from Nathan, excoriating us because we hadn't had a
proper bris.

Ben: Megan had called half a dozen rabbis, but they wouldn't come to
the hospital to do the bris because she wasn't Jewish. So it's not like we
hadn't tried.

Megan: So Ben walked in and saw me holding the letter and just crying
my eyes out. He came over and took the letter out of my hand and read it;
then he picked up the phone and called home and his mother answered,
and he just said, "Is Dad home? I need to talk to him."

And he said to his dad, "We got your letter. This decision was our decision to make. This is our family. You have no right to tell us how to raise
our children. My wife is sitting here in tears and I'm going to put her on
the phone and I expect you to apologize to her." So I'm across the room
frantically signaling, "No, no, don't put me on the phone with him!" and
Ben hands me the phone. So I took the phone and said, "Hi," and he said,

"Hi Megan, this is Nathan. I'm very sorry if I upset you. I didn't mean to do that and I'm sorry." I said, "Okay, apology accepted," and that was the last time he ever tried to interfere.

I cannot tell you how important that was. It was a defining moment in our relationship. I will never forget—I can see Ben's face in my mind. It was the first time he stood up to his father, and I didn't feel so crazy and so alone. And he's never asked me to accommodate his father more than I could. And when he overstepped like that, Ben just stopped it. So when Nathan was annoying at other times, it was a lot easier for me to just let it go.

I've tried to be really respectful of his family. He's my husband and I need to figure this out. If we didn't have a strong relationship, it would have been harder. For a long time I was seen as the rabble-rouser, but it's much better now. One of Ben's sisters still acts like Nathan is a saint, and you can't even hint that maybe he had a couple of flaws.

It also really helped that when I was puzzled or upset by something in Ben's family I could just ask him about it, not in an angry way, but just because I didn't understand. And he might get defensive for a while, but then he'd always come back and say, "I've been thinking about what you said, and I think you have a point."

Ben: Don't forget, you were pointing out things that were completely normal in my family, that I grew up with, that nobody ever questioned! You also got more diplomatic when you asked about certain things too, and that helped. It does make a difference when someone asks questions like that if they can be gentle about it. She made it easier for me not to get defensive, which was my natural reaction sometimes.

How have the two of you been able to deal together with Elias's illness? Has that been a problem between the two of you?

Megan: We don't get to choose what genes we pass on to our children. One of the kids got my bad eyesight, and one of them got this mental illness. I know it makes Ben feel guilty, but I don't think there's any blame involved. We had to come out of our own denial before we got to set some good boundaries, like when we said to Elias, "Yes, you have this illness, but you still have to learn to manage your life. We'll help you but you have to do your part too. Everybody has to learn how to manage their own life and their own problems."

What would you both say to somebody with a similar in-law situation who might want your input?

Ben: Talk a lot and listen well.

Megan: When in doubt, go to your relationship. Don't blame your spouse for their family's stuff. The marriage has to be your ally; it has to be central.

Ben: Give your spouse a safe place to talk about what's happening for them in your family. Try not to be judgmental about any of it. What you choose to do now is much more important than where you came from or what's happened in the past.

Megan: I have to remember that this is his family.

Ben: And I have to remember that she and the kids are my family now, and that they come first.

ABOUT BEN: MY REFLECTIONS

A central problem Ben has faced is that his father was so contradictory: loving and attentive at some times, but also self-centered, demanding, and even frightening. These diametrically opposed traits have so far defied integration. Where things went well between Ben and his father, it was undoubtedly possible partly because Ben is himself gifted artistically and was naturally fascinated by his father's world; a musical child, for example, with different interests and talents, might have had a much harder time.

Ben maintained his good family connection partly by buying into the code of Protect Dad at All Costs. This put him on the same side as his mother, and he also simply "knew" that he couldn't talk to her about his own struggles with his father. So there was loyalty and solidarity, which kept the family tightly bound together but at some cost. Ben's marriage to Megan changed the family dynamic quite a bit; that's one of the benefits of having an outside perspective. They've had to learn how to honor Ben's connection with his father without leaving Ben's wife and kids in second place. And as Ben and his wife said, they've put the marriage first, without disrespect for the in-laws.

Ben struggles not only with integrating different parts of his father but also with being able to think "disloyal" thoughts inside his own head. In the interview, whenever he expressed negative feelings about his father, he would quickly turn the conversation back to his father's wonderful qualities. His wish not to be like his father in holding grudges has made it hard for him to acknowledge old hurts and injuries, and he wants to "let things go" before they're sufficiently resolved.

This is one of two men (Patrick is the other) in this book who found out, in their late teens or early 20s, about their fathers' affairs with other women. For both men it's been hard to go back and think of this as a factor in understanding their families and especially their mothers. The fact of these affairs, and the wives' knowledge of them, made it easier for me to understand their apparent distance from their husbands, their silence on such topics as how they held the family together, and the cost to themselves. For Ben's mother, one area of silence was her husband's illness, and another area would have been his infidelity.

The fact of Ben's son being diagnosed with the father's illness has been painful, yet I think Ben's approach to being there for his son is an admirable accomplishment, pragmatically and emotionally. Ben and his wife were generous in sharing their approach and their thinking about this very difficult topic, and I can't add to what they can teach us from their own experience.

WHAT CAN WE LEARN FROM BEN'S STORY?

Ben's story helps us remember that a parent who's inconsistent can be both confusing and helpful. Ben's father is, on the one hand, brilliant and highly acclaimed for his artistic achievements. On the other hand, he might have ended up homeless had his wife and his academic job not protected him from his excesses. These are really very extreme swings and that makes it hard to put them all in one package. His erratic, self-centered, over-the-top behavior seems very at odds with his closeness to his son at other times.

It's especially hard for a child to make sense of all this when the family rule is to be silent about it. His mother certainly held the family together very admirably, yet at a cost. The difficulties were simply ignored, as though there was nothing to discuss. When Ben's wife, an outside observer, comes on the scene, she is able to say, "The Emperor has no clothes." It's easy to be blinded by loyalty and familiarity, and important to have an outside view sometimes. If Ben or his siblings had been included in his father's treatment or informed about his diagnosis, it would have made it possible to talk more openly and freely and might have taken some of the burden off his mother. It also might have made it easier for Ben to integrate his contradictory feelings about his complicated and challenging father.

6

Thomas: "She must have hundreds of cuts on her body"

Thomas lives in Canada and grew up with his parents, brother, and sister. His family seemed pretty normal to him, except for his own temper problems, until he was 10 and came home to find that his mother had made a suicide attempt. From that point on there was a series of mental hospitals, and years of his mother's unsuccessful treatment, leading to his parents' divorce and his living with another family for a couple of years. Thomas is unusual in that he talked about his family to anyone who would listen, and he was given a great deal of professional support regarding his mother's illness. He's now in his early 30s and is happy that his mother has recovered and the family has reconnected.

Can you tell me a little about where you grew up, who was in the family, that sort of thing?

I grew up in a small community in rural western Canada. It's your traditional small-town community where you are loosely connected to everyone, but this isn't to say there isn't also family privacy.

I'm the youngest of three children. My sister is five years older, and my brother is two years older. My dad worked in television when I was growing up, and my mom worked for an insurance company. Mom apparently didn't do this job very long into my life, because I believe she had her first "breakdown" when I was two years old (although this was all kept a secret from the children). She stopped working around that time.

What was your mom like when you were younger, before you were aware of her emotional problems?

Quite honestly, I remember her being a very supportive mother. One time specifically I remember her coming to my third-grade class and helping with a multicultural day. She used to come to all of our sporting events. I didn't really have any idea that anything was going on with her whatsoever.

She would get us ready for school, and she'd make dinner; she did all the things that moms do during the day when dads are at work and kids are at school. She changed our house a lot—the furniture, the wallpaper, the knick-knacks—it seemed like our home theme was always changing! Looking back, maybe it was an outlet for some of her anxiety.

Did you feel pretty close to her?

Not necessarily really emotionally close, even though I remember things like her going to a lot of trouble to give great birthday parties for me, making really cool cakes, and whatnot. But I mostly have those positive memories I already mentioned, and there's not much else. I don't really have a warm feeling about her back then. We didn't have any incredible bond per se. She was very emotionally reserved in a way I can't really put my finger on. So I kind of have some nice memories and I know she did a lot of things right, but I don't think I felt especially close to her in the way you mean it.

But I can tell you I am comforted by thoughts of my mom singing at church. She had such a beautiful voice, I thought. My mom used to rock me to sleep when I was really young, and when she did that she'd sing to me, and that's a very nice memory.

Were there things that happened in your family that you thought of as "just the way it is" that you learned later were different from other families?

For the most part we really were your typical family until "the day." I think the main thing in our family was that I was a super volatile personality. I fought with my dad all the time; I was just averse to authority in general: teachers, principals, parents—it didn't matter. I couldn't sit still, and when someone told me to settle down, I wasn't interested in hearing about it. I would throw the hugest fits over nothing, and my dad would try to put me in my room and then we'd get in huge fights, and my mom would try to step in and I'd turn on her, but she often was the one who separated the fights. I'd get locked in my room and I'd scream and scream; then when I had nothing left my dad would come in and calmly tell me he still loved me.

What was the explanation for your anger and temper? Were you seen as having problems or being difficult on purpose?

I definitely was seen as having problems, and I am pretty sure everyone would have thought it was on purpose. At the time no one really understood what was wrong with me; they all just thought I had really bad ADHD, which I was diagnosed with eventually. I craved attention, bad—in public, in school, anywhere I was. It's strange, because now I am much more reserved, almost the complete opposite of my child self.

How did that go over with your brother and sister?

My brother and I were best friends before all the stuff started to happen with my mom. We did everything together—hung out with the same friends, dressed the same, played the same sports—we literally were best friends.

My sister, being five years older, always seemed to view me as very immature, and rightfully so. It seems as though we fought more than we did anything else together. Once she invited a bunch of friends over and I was acting up as usual, and so they tied me up with belts. Well, I was claustrophobic, so I freaked out! So she gave me milk, which I later learned was laced with Tylenol because she thought it would subdue me. So I guess you could say we weren't all that close!

How did you and your dad work these things out? It sounds like he was pretty tough but also kept trying to find a way to make things better with you.

Actually, Dad was pretty much my hero. I just wanted to be as tall and strong as he was. He coached all our sports teams and he was always there to watch us play sports. But outside of sports, our relationship at home was strained as I mentioned above. He also had a temper, and I set it off pretty often.

So, when was the first time you knew something was wrong with your mom?

One day we were a perfect little family, and then that just came apart all at once. When I was 10, I came home from school and there was a cop car at my house, and they put me in the police car and I was asking what's going on. I don't think the officer realized, but I could read his clipboard and I saw "attempted suicide." I was completely shocked, but I still didn't understand. My dad was with my sister at a softball game, and my brother was probably out with his friends somewhere. The police officer drove me miles and miles and miles looking for my father (nobody had cell phones then), and when we found him we pulled him over, and then we had a movie moment right there on the side of the highway. I ran to him and burst into tears and he hugged me, and that's when his world came crashing down in front of him.

My dad didn't understand what had happened at first. Actually, his initial reaction was "What did Thomas do?" I went to the car, and then Dad came back after he talked to the police officer. Dad told me what had happened and that my mom was sick. My sister had known for years, as we had made a trip to Vancouver when we were quite young so my mom could spend a few weeks in the psych ward of a major hospital. My brother and I were so young at the time, we didn't understand why we were in Vancouver or why Mom wasn't around, but my sister knew because she was that much older. So she understood all along that Mom was sick, but I don't think she or my dad knew it would progress to cutting. We all went to visit Mom in the hospital, our first of many, many trips to visit Mom in the psych ward. We were told that she was abused by her father, and over the years more of these stories were shared with us, very horrible things, things that to this day make me want to hurt this man, but he died before I was old enough to find out about any of this. I hate this man and have not spoken a single word to his wife (our "ahem" grandmother) since she stormed out of our house when I was four. I didn't know it then, but I assume the argument was about the abuse or something. Sadly, my brother and sister and I will never speak to her for the rest of her life. We do not consider that side of our family to be "family." The things that were done in that household are horrific, intolerable, unimaginable and bring me to anger nearly 18 years since they first came to light.

Did she tell you about her abuse, or did a professional explain it? What sense did you make of it?

My mother did not tell me, no. This is a really tough one to draw on, because going back then just reminds me of the terrible things that people do to their children. No, a professional explained it to us. I was very angry; I didn't understand how the world could be so ugly. I knew it wasn't my mom's fault now—she was a victim, and in essence my family was a victim of a terrible person. I never blamed her, but for some reason my brother and sister have had a lot harder time with it and took a long time to get over being so angry at her.

Were the mental health professionals helpful at all? Did they help you make sense of it?

Family therapy was incredibly helpful to me. The older I get the more I realize how important it was right at that time. I think it was less about trying to shelter me or protect me from what was happening, but more an opportunity for me to express and really open up a verbal dialogue where I could go through a sort of self-guided process and feel safe to cry and cry and cry. I cried a lot of those sessions, and I'm not embarrassed to say it. (Ha ha!)

What was life like in the family after "the day" and during the time your mom was going in and out of the hospital?

Mom wasn't very functional at all, to be honest. She was cutting more and more, and so all the knives were removed from the house; but she would buy X-acto knives when she was out shopping and she'd hide those. My sister would have to look under her bed to make sure she wasn't hiding any there. But it didn't matter—Mom would always find some tool to scratch or cut herself with regardless of what we did. I remember clear as day, she carved the word "cut" into the wall beside her bed. It's a memory that haunts me to this day. I would bet she has thousands of cuts on her body. And she's a small woman!

She was in and out of the hospital for weeks at a time. We'd go visit her, read her letters we wrote, have family meetings with a therapist in the hospital, everything. To this day hospitals aren't the most pleasant experience for any of us. When she wasn't in the hospital, she was in bed. It was literally like this for years. Once I went to check on her at night, as us kids often did to make sure she hadn't hurt herself or taken too many pills, and I must have triggered something because she let out the most blood-curdling scream I can imagine. It was horrific—another memory that haunts me to this day. I just had to keep repeating, "Mom, it's me, Thomas; Mom, it's Thomas." During this time we lost our car to debt, and my dad lost his job because my mom's health problems took him away from work too often. She wasn't making any effort to get better, just simply relying on him to save her over and over again.

What was going on between her and your father during this time?

It almost seemed like the more disruption she caused with all the emergencies, the worse she got until it totally controlled my dad's life. He would have to race home at whatever hour of the day because she called him at work in tears. It impacted his ability to do his job, and I remember this period was like the worst. He had lost so much—his wife, his home, his car—and he just kept hanging around and doing what he could to try and keep the family together while she didn't even come out of her room. I wanted him to leave. I could tell he had had enough; he was growing more and more frustrated with her each day. I remember one fight very clearly where he lost his temper, and I just stood there in our living room and told him to leave our house.

How did he and your mom get along with each other prior to all this?

I'm not sure. I think they did okay before all that stuff happened; but when money went sideways, they used to get into arguments in front of me or in my earshot. Later on when Mom was at her worst, my dad just wanted her to get better. Eventually, he felt that she wasn't trying to get better, and she was just more and more relying on him to get by. He was in a loveless relationship for so long and he just couldn't do it anymore.

Did you and your siblings go through this together, emotionally?

When we were sat down to discuss things as a family, or had to go to the hospital to have a family session, then yeah, we were there together; but I certainly felt very disconnected from a collective emotional wavelength, and I am sure my siblings would say the same. We all just sort of lived our lives to the best of our ability with what was going on with Mom.

I told you me and my brother had been extremely close, best friends, when we were kids. This changed entirely after "the day." Suddenly my brother became very reserved from the family, spent very little time at home, and showed no emotion. When I was moved out of the home to live with the other family, both he and my sister resented me. We were still brothers, we were connected by a great cause, but we certainly did not have the relationship we once did.

Were you talking to anyone about this during that time? Did you know or spend time with that other family at that age, and were they helpful?

Because of my willingness to share, and the fact that this to me was just a part of life, it just was what it was at the time. My friends would see my mom being stretchered out of the house when we walked home from school, and I'd sit them down and explain it to them. We'd spend Christmas in the psych ward of the hospital, but we were visiting a sick woman. I understand now why I was so volatile in the house. I was picking up a lot of the tension between my parents and I was just pushing it to the explosion point.

I was always open with all of my friends about my life—I didn't hide anything—and it's something I feel was a very important thing to do for me then. I was in youth group and spoke with the youth pastor pretty often, and I still had a lot of therapy at the time. The other family was just coming into my life, but they wanted to give me a normal, stable home rather than being a place where we talked about this all the time. When things progressed they were always there to talk with me and ensure I was exploring what happened.

Before you left to live with the other family, how did you cope?

I stayed away from home as long as I could. After school I would go to a friend's and get home at 8:00 p.m. I wouldn't even call and I was only 10 or 11. Silly boy, I guess, but it sort of says something about the respect or understanding I had about the parent role. It sort of disappeared the moment I realized that parents weren't perfect; they were just older versions of me, with their own problems. This was both a blessing and a curse to have learned this when I did.

I coped by talking it out with my friends, talking in therapy, and doing sports. I just wanted to be a normal kid and so I tried to normalize what was happening with my mom as if every kid was going through it.

This was all until I was 14 and in the ninth grade. That's when my father started the process of leaving my mother, and when he initially left the household, I was sent to live with this other family, who we loosely knew through our church. I lived with this family for a short time but then moved back in with my mother. One night I checked on my mom in her bedroom to make sure she was okay, and she seemed as though she had taken too many pills. She was slurring her speech and not making much sense, and I was the only one in the house with her. So I called the other family to come help me out, and I got my mom out of bed and kept her awake by making her pass a basketball back and forth with me until they came. For the second time it was decided it was best for me to move back in with them, and this time I lived with them for the remainder of my ninth-grade and all of my tenth-grade year. My sister moved out of the house after she graduated, leaving my brother living with my mom alone from when he was 15 on until he moved away.

Who decided that you should live with this other family—who was involved in that? What was it like for you? What happened to your mom?

The other family I was connected to through our church youth group. My dad worked it out with them, and they told me as a group. I don't know what the conversation looked like or what precipitated it; all I know is that because Dad was leaving Mom and I was the youngest, they didn't think it was good for me to live with just my mom. I also was a bit of a problem child, so I guess they probably didn't think she was going to be able to handle it if I acted up, nor did they know what direction my life would go if I was left entirely unsupervised. It was the right decision and I was very happy with the other family. They were so peaceful, the house was soooo quiet compared to ours, and they rarely turned the TV on. They owned a ranch that was 30 minutes from town and so I had 2,300 acres to run around on. I learned to change the engine of a truck and feed horses and I could go on forever. These people were absolute angels.

At some point it was decided I should live with my dad, and I still don't think it was fair that I wasn't involved in that decision. I had been moved around a lot and I felt like nobody wanted me. My mom was still living at home.

A big thing for me was when I realized that parents weren't perfect and they had problems just like anyone else. My relationship with my dad really grew after "the day," in spite of telling him once in ninth grade, "Don't try to parent me. You're not 'the father'—you're just a man."

It did help that there was always that other family, and they encouraged me to ask questions and made sure I knew what was going on. I'm incredibly lucky that I had this encouragement from people to express myself and just deal with stuff as it came up.

What kinds of problems did you have apart from being angry and having temper outbursts?

I was afraid of everything. The dark, going to sleep, walking home by myself—everything scared me. I ran a lot. When things were tense, I poked the bear. I still do to this day. I have an awful habit of prodding and prodding until things explode. When I was nervous I would push things even more. That's one reason it was so good for me to be with that other family where things were basically calm and I could calm down and get involved in a lot of things I liked doing.

Was your family involved with other people, relatives, neighbors?

My parents were always involved in our church, and a lot of our social circle was people from the church. But when my mom got sick they weren't supportive, and my parents decided to leave that church and move to another. And I think that was an excellent decision and has helped my mom.

How did things go as you got older?

Well, I never did finish high school, but I've built a good sales career and have been involved in community leadership for the past five or six years. I have pretty good "emotional intelligence" because of what I went through. My mom is doing extremely well and just turned a corner. Her story is a story of perseverance, one that needs to be told, as after she was victimized as a child, she was revictimized as an adult. She lost everything for a while, even her family, but she never gave up; she worked with her doctors, her support workers, and with God, and just recently I cried when she told me she is only on one medication a day, an antidepressant. She's stronger than ever. She's gained her family back, and I love her so desperately. She is my rock and a lesson to the world that no matter how awful, how evil, how horrific things can be, you can get through it. I'm emotional writing this part because I just can't express enough the difference in my mom. I have a mom again when I never thought I would.

I think you probably realize how remarkable that is. How about your dad and brother and sister? How are they doing?

Dad remarried, and we're best friends now. We see the world in a very similar way, and we have formed such an incredible bond. We had that back when I was a kid too. I respect him so much for everything he went through, and his story is also one of perseverance and bouncing back. He moved away right when I would have graduated high school—the exact same day as the ceremony actually—no joke. He paid the rent on our basement apartment, then he told me to get a job or get out. I've forgiven him for that one. He got his degree and has become quite a successful leader as well. He is such a good guy, everyone's favorite kind of person now—he transcends generations. I even had the opportunity to work side by side in an organization with him for a few years. So cool.

My brother has just turned an important corner. He's decided what he really wants to do, and he got into school and is pursuing that. He was always the one most connected to Mom, and my idea is, when she started getting well he started to get himself together too. He has more confidence than I've seen in him in a long time.

My sister is the proud mother of a two-year-old and this is the role she absolutely loves. She tried her best to mother my brother and me when Mom got sick, and she definitely revels in that role! She has taken the longest to forgive Mom, but she also lived through it the longest, so it may be understandable. She was the only one who knew Mom was sick and had to deal with it long before my brother and me.

Do you and your mother ever talk about it? Does she acknowledge that she had problems or has it not been okay to talk about?

We've never talked about it. The only conversations I've ever had with my mom regarding her mental health are always when I'm encouraging her to reach for health. Like I said, when she told me she was only on one medication, after all she's been through, I cried. But that's the most we would say. She's a beautiful woman, and I love her; but no, we did not ever discuss her issues. *Everything* was a trigger for her; she couldn't go to the movie theater without being triggered by something. The last thing I ever wanted to do was be the cause of one of her downswings.

How did you turn the corner yourself, and how do you think your family members did as well?

I think for me and for all of us, it's simply that the turning point continues, each and every day. We all make conscious or subconscious decisions to keep making the right decisions, to grow as people, and to work to rebuild the bonds of family.

We are living our turning points now, and we'll continue to live them for the rest of our lives. If anybody reading this is hoping that a silver bullet exists, I truly and honestly do not believe there is one thing that can be the breakthrough for everyone. For me it all begins with an unwillingness to be a victim and a willingness to grow. And it made all the difference in the world to see the separation between Mom and her "disease." That allowed us to forgive her and see her more as a woman and a mother and less of a villain. She still needs support in her healing and doesn't need people who are angry with her or blame her for their life not being a fantasy storyboard.

It's really been a pleasure sharing this with you, and if my story touches the heart of one person struggling with their own difficulties, then this process has served me 10 times over. And I did ask my brother and sister if they wanted to add anything, and my brother sent me this:

> Thomas's brother: I am not very good at writing my feelings, but I'm going to give this my best shot. A big part of the reason I feel like my life didn't go down the tubes is that I had a good support system. If it weren't for my brother, sister, and father especially, I probably wouldn't be the person I am today. I think that Dad being somebody I could look up to, and strive to be, was huge. I saw him going through all the crises with Mom, and raising us kids and holding down a job. It made a big impression on me, and it made me feel that if he could do that, I could try my hardest to be a normal functioning person too.
>
> As far as a turning point, it would have to be the day a friend and I came home to find Mom in the bedroom, unconscious and not responding, with four empty bottles of pills on the ground. That night absolutely freaked me out. I can honestly say I was not the same person from that day forward. [He was 16.]
>
> We went to the hospital as a family and told her she would not be in our lives if she didn't get her act together. I believe that was the turning point in my relationship with Mom. I moved away for two years, and it gave her time to work out her issues, without us being there to rescue her all the time. It also gave me time to heal some of my

wounds and to get away from the people I had surrounded myself with, and also get away from the drug scene.

It has taken at least 12 years to get to the point I am at today with Mom, but she proves more and more to me every day that she deserves my love. I am very happy that she is the person she is today. She's the mother I always wanted and needed. I can say that forgiving her for what we went through has been the hardest yet most fulfilling thing I have ever experienced in my life. I would also say that these things take time, but forgiving is the best thing you can do to fix yourself. I love my family very much and wouldn't trade them for anything in the world.

ABOUT THOMAS: MY REFLECTIONS

Thomas's story is unusual in that he seemed to have expressed himself nonstop for as long as he can remember. His frequent tantrums and outbursts were certainly a strain on his family when he was a child, but his insistence on talking when his mother got sick was life-saving for him. We don't hear him talking about shame or silence or isolation; in fact, he explained things to his school friends when they asked questions, and talked to the family that took him in when he was a teenager as well as talking to professionals.

It's also unusual for a family to have so many professional resources, especially family therapy that seems to have gone on for a long time. He can say with authority that he needed a place to talk, to vent, to cry, and to be accepted as he went through the family crises. (It's worth reiterating that Thomas is Canadian, and Canada, Australia, and the Netherlands are three countries that have a great awareness of, and very generous resources for, the families of mentally ill patients.)

He also had an alternative family to live with, and a church family for support, both of which were very important factors in getting him through this tough time. And despite the divorce, his father remained involved with his children and helped to make their lives more manageable. It seemed clear to Thomas that his father was divorcing his mother for understandable reasons and that Thomas didn't feel abandoned in the process.

Part of Thomas's recovery has to do with his mother's dramatic improvement. Her cutting and other self-injury, as well as suicide attempts, are common symptoms associated with incest, and they are treatable. In the past she might have been diagnosed incorrectly (e.g., as schizophrenic) and had a lifetime of symptoms and chronic misery. She seems to have recovered, with a lot of hard work, and she and her children have a much-improved relationship. This is a happier ending than we have seen in many of these stories.

WHAT CAN WE LEARN FROM THOMAS'S STORY?

His story includes a lot of the right things adults can do in the face of a series of mental health crises. When the problems surfaced, all the children were told what was wrong and why. Telling a child about a parent's having been sexually abused is a hard call to make, but in this case it helped Thomas demystify what was happening and doubtless prevented him from feeling guilty or responsible for his mother's problems.

The family had a lot of professional help and that seemed to help quite a bit. There was also another place for Thomas to live, where he was free to talk about these things but also to have a more normal growing-up period doing a lot of things that were good for him. Again, no secrecy was required, and there was a lot of opportunity to have a life apart from the family without having to pretend the problems didn't still exist. Shame and stigma seem to be absent from this story.

The family also felt able to make some boundaries when it seemed they were needed, like telling their mother that she had to get her act together and take treatment seriously. If this family had all stayed together, trying to rescue Mom in a vacuum, it could have imploded.

7

Brian: "Just understand your father, for my sake"

Brian is a young man whose father has been difficult to understand and deal with throughout Brian's life. His mother asks that Brian "make allowances" for his dad, but Brian's reaction growing up was to be "the cold one." He's recently ended a three-year relationship and has sought therapy to help him understand how his history has affected him emotionally. His father has never been diagnosed or treated but has some peculiar behaviors and has not been able to connect emotionally to his children.

You've said that your father has some kind of emotional problem that hasn't been diagnosed. What's the first memory you have of him?

I remember when I was really young, maybe three or four, I ran into my mother's room, and I was really upset and told her I was afraid that my father and brother would kill me. She comforted me, but I remember being truly frightened. I was definitely wary of my dad. He would tease me and it would seem like things were okay, and then he would lash out. He punched me a few times, and I know he was more violent with my older brother and sister.

I know when I was 9 or 10 that he had this overwhelming anger most of the time. He was scary. I had heard that when he was a child, his family had financial problems and the authorities came and took everything out of the house, while the family had to stand there and watch. I had also heard that his parents were very physically abusive to him. Even the most minor infraction of their rules—like stepping into the yard without permission—would get him a beating. As he told it, his parents wore big rings on their hands and made a point that it would hurt more that way. So it seems like they were really kind of deliberately cruel to him.

So I knew even when I was younger that he had a hard time growing up, but some of the stuff he did just wasn't normal. For example, he was always counting the silverware and the cups and plates in the kitchen. And it's not like this was expensive or valuable; it was just regular household stuff. So anytime anything was missing or not in the exact right place, or God forbid scratched or broken, he would go around the house confronting one person after the other, saying, "Did you do this? Did you take this? Did you put this here?"

I remember feeling really anxious as a kid; there was just a lot of background anxiety around him. I would dread hearing his footsteps coming up the stairs. He would knock on the door, and it wasn't, "Can I come in?" It was, "Head's up, I'm coming in." I'll never forget him going up the stairs after my brother when my brother was saying, "No, don't come up here." My dad went in his room, and I could hear him beating my brother and hearing the crying through the closed door. My mother wasn't around to make sure he didn't do it.

I used to think my mom should just divorce him, and I told her that when I was in high school. She didn't want to talk about it. It was a very hard thing to say to her because I usually kept my mouth shut.

So you didn't really understand what was setting him off or what your brother did that made him angry. Did he get angry with you as well?

Growing up I was known as the "cold-hearted one." I didn't show emotion, or I would just act flippant. My dad is really strange, because if he gets worked up about something, he just starts bitching about it and he can't stop. It goes on and on. He used to come in my room when I was doing homework or on my computer and he would start complaining about something. I would completely ignore him and he would just keep going. If he started focusing on me or bitching about something I was doing, I would just sit there and try to zone out. He would just obsess endlessly about whatever it was. Eventually, he would stop and then he would go away. I could just sit through the entire thing and never say one word. I know people can get worked up about things, but this just isn't normal.

So you didn't have any anxiety that if you ignored him or tried to tune him out, he would think you were being rude or insolent?

Hmm. That never crossed my mind. He never reacted that way.

Some parents wouldn't tolerate that kind of reaction. It would seem rude to them and things would get more intense, not less. Did you feel intimidated by him?

No, not by the time I was a teenager. He would just go on and on until he ran out of gas, then he would walk out of my room. I know he could lash out kind of impulsively, but this seemed different. He just couldn't stop himself.

Were there some good times with him, when you and he did things together or he was helpful or seemed more connected?

Playing tennis with him was okay when I was a kid, until I got to where I could beat him most of the time. In middle school my mom might guilt him into helping us with school projects, but it always ended up with his being angry. I remember feeling miserable and just standing there watching. It wasn't, "Let's do this together." It was, "Watch me while I angrily try to get this to work." You watch and you endure.

Other times he might ask me to help him do something in the yard, like rake the leaves. But it was the same thing. If you didn't do it exactly precisely the way he wanted it done, he would scream and yell and just be irrational. There was really no point in trying. I mean, this was beyond being particular about how he wanted something done—it was just irrational.

What was a typical kind of day for you when you were younger, in elementary school?

My mom worked, but she was usually home when we got home. Her mom was around a lot, and we all got along really well. I felt close to my mom and could talk to her, and it was a good feeling when my dad wasn't there. He came home late and I would try to avoid him, but we had to have dinner together as a family.

What was that like?

The mood would always be tense. He might start going off about something, and my brother would get into it with him. My sister would just start to cry. But I was "the cold one," the one made out of stone, because I wouldn't react—I would just disconnect. I would try to ignore whatever my dad was doing. I just acted like nothing was going on. Everybody thought I had no feelings whatsoever. I would think, to both my brother and sister—"Why don't you just shut up? This isn't going to help anything; we don't have any control over this at all. There's no point. You're ultimately going to have to adjust to them because they're not going to change."

How did things change when you became a teenager?

My dad and I were taking the dogs out once, and out of nowhere, just standing in the backyard, he just tells me, "I shouldn't have married your mother." I was only about 14 and it's not something he should be saying to his kid. I didn't say anything to him, but it felt pretty bad. I also thought he would never do anything about it. He would just wallow in it. He's a very negative person and he complains a lot. I'm sure that if he and my mom ever actually split up, he wouldn't know what to do, because he doesn't have any friends.

So I can't actually imagine him without my mom and I actually can't imagine her without him either. She does have a lot of friends, but I don't know how she'd manage financially. One thing he's always done well is to provide financially for us, and I do appreciate that and know that means a lot to him too.

How did your brother and sister deal with things at home during those years, when they were older teenagers and you were a few years younger?

My brother suffered from depression through high school and also into college. I know my sister did too to some extent, but his seemed more severe. He was on various kinds of medication and it took him a few years to get off them. He's better now. My dad was kind of skeptical about it all and would say critical things to me about my brother like, "he's just doing that for attention." I didn't think he should be saying that kind of thing to me because he's the parent. It felt wrong, and I also thought my brother was really pretty depressed and my father didn't realize it. My brother stayed to himself after a while; he just isolated himself and played video games. I used to wish he would just come out of his room.

When I got to high school and I got bigger, there came a point where I said to my dad once when he just hit me in the shoulder, "If you do that to me again I'm going to lay you out. I'm old enough to fight back, you know." I was 15 when I said that to him, and he stopped after that.

My brother handled it differently. He was home from college and something happened and my father hit him on the arm. But my brother just kind of smiled and didn't even react; it was like he was thinking, "This is just funny at this point." My mom was upset, but he wasn't.

Did your dad ever embarrass you when you were growing up?

He was really socially awkward. Like he's still very shy when it comes to meeting new people. He doesn't really know how to help carry the conversation or keep things going and he's very nervous. But in a conversation you can tell he's not really processing what's going on and not really listening to what people are saying, because if there's a joke or reference to something, he might not even get it. He might laugh as though he did get it, but you could tell that he really didn't.

Did you have friends come over to your house, or did you avoid that?

I only had a couple of close friends in elementary school where they would sleep over, so I spent more time at other people's houses rather than their being at my house. In high school or middle school, almost in spite of him I would have friends over and I didn't care. I realized that he had a problem and it was his to deal with and I wasn't going to let it run my life. I don't mean he would say no if I asked him, but I was determined not to avoid hanging out with my friends at my house just because he might act weird.

How did your friends react to him?

I don't remember them saying too much, but if I would say something like, "My dad is kind of nuts," they would say, "Yeah." But I remember one time, when some friends and I were going up to Vermont and my parents were coming too. My mom and dad were in one car, and my friends and I were in the other car, and my friend opened the car door at the same time my dad opened the car door and the doors touched. Now my father is completely obsessive about his car. He could tell you every ding and every scratch—he could tell you the date he got it and exactly how he got it. So these two doors touched and my father went completely apeshit. And my friend said, "You told me about your father, but I've never seen it until today. Holy shit!" And it was clearly a moment where my dad couldn't help himself. And of course there was absolutely nothing on the door. The doors just barely touched. And later on he apologized like he always does. But over the years his apologies mean less and less to me because they're never followed by any action. He never tries to change what he's doing. I don't think he even knows what he's apologizing for. He seems to feel bad if he upsets someone else, but he really doesn't comprehend why they're upset.

So at that point, you weren't worrying that you were the one responsible for his reactions. You don't seem to have been thinking that you should be able to keep him calm and prevent that kind of thing from happening?

I think when I was younger I really took it to heart and thought about what I could do to make things work better. I don't know the exact point when things changed, but it was eighth grade or ninth grade when I just thought, "He's acting like a kid." I think my brother and sister took his behavior to heart more than I did by then.

So if somebody said to you, "Look, this isn't your fault; your father has a serious problem," you wouldn't feel relieved. You'd be more likely to think, "Yeah, what else is new? I knew that. What are you going to do about it?"

Exactly. These are his problems. I didn't cause them and I can't even help with them. It's not my fault he won't get help and he won't try even to recognize what he's doing. My sister still feels kind of responsible and tiptoes around him.

What was it like to be around other adult men: teachers, coaches, your friends' fathers?

I do find myself even now as an adult latching onto strong personalities and then trying to meet their expectations. When I was a kid it was my tennis coach, when I was playing a lot of tennis and getting pretty good. Then I got into music and had a male music teacher, and that heavily influenced my high school career because I honestly thought at that time that I would become a musician. I wanted to meet their expectations and I wanted to go above and beyond.

Now that you're an adult, how is your relationship with your parents? How are they doing with each other?

They're still together and I think my mom has better boundaries about what she'll put up with and what she won't. And he seems a little bit more aware of who he is and what he's doing, especially with other people.

How are you dealing with them these days, then?

I've been more confrontational with both my parents since I graduated from college and especially in the last year, and part of that is probably because I've been talking to a therapist too. I've been living in their in-law apartment and paying rent to them. A couple of months ago, my dad and I got into an argument about something dumb—I think maybe about a problem with the Internet access—and I just tried to leave the room after it was obvious it was going nowhere, but he followed me and kept going because by then he was all worked up about it. So he's following me and he's yelling at me, and by this time I'm breaking down and I'm crying and I don't really have any choice about where to go. So I couldn't disconnect like I always have in the past; he was kind of forcing me to deal with it. So for the first time I just lashed out. I just lost it and I kept yelling at him, "You just need to shut the fuck up. You just need to shut the fuck up." And he was like a deer in the headlights because no one ever sees me like that. I am the emotionless one. I'm the cold one who never reacts. And I was hitting the couch and I just kept saying to him, "You need to shut up. I just can't deal with this anymore." I was crying by that point and I just walked into my room and slammed the door.

That's a pretty intense situation and really different for you. How did you feel afterwards?

Actually, I felt pretty good at that point. Why do I always need to be the one who's flexible?

Good point.

I've been more confrontational with my mom too. She doesn't really have an outlet or anyone to talk to about it, and in the last year or so there have been some pretty emotional conversations between us and she's expressed her unhappiness. She's not happy with the situation because it's like a constant battle. The reality is, what would either of them do without the other? My mom just keeps saying, "We've got our issues, but every family has its issues." But when we talk about it, it's validating to me—it's not a burden. It helps me understand it better. She never bad-mouths my father, but she might say she wishes they could work things out more easily. The thing that's been the hardest for me is when she makes us go and apologize to him when he's been the one in the wrong.

Do you think that's just the way things have to be? That you just understand his limitations and work around them for the most part?

Well, it's not always that clear-cut. Like, he's just a horrible driver sometimes. We went on a family trip last year and we were in a kind of remote mountainous area, and we were there in the car and he was driving on these very narrow, twisty winding roads. He knew that the last time we were on vacation together and he drove like that I had been very upset. And like I said, I know he doesn't like to feel he's upset somebody. So I thought maybe he would listen and I asked him to slow down. And he got all defensive. And my aunt and my mother in the car kept saying to him, "We're not worried about your driving; we're worried about the other drivers." But I was thinking, "I'm not worried about the other drivers; I'm worried about *him*." But I finally thought, "This is out of my hands," and so I just put my earbuds in and sat back and rode it out. Thank goodness I wasn't in the front seat. And again later he apologized to me, but I don't know what he was apologizing for.

So for once I actually spoke up. I objected to what he was doing and it still didn't work.

How did the others in the car react? Were you in serious danger?

Yeah, we were. Absolutely. There was another passenger in the car, a girl about 10 or 11 years old, and when we got out of the car my mom said, "I think Julie should get a medal for being the best passenger in the car because she didn't complain about anything." That was a direct shot at me. So I objected to that and she said, "I just wish you could understand your father and cut him some slack." So basically there's just this pressure to give more, like why can't you just understand him, just not push him like that. So I said, "Look, that was unacceptable, and if there had been a car coming the opposite direction, *three separate times*, we would've been dead." She just said, "I don't want to talk about this right now, and I just wish you could understand him and do it for my sake."

* * *

It's been a couple of weeks since the first interview. Did you have any thoughts or reactions afterwards?

Yeah, just talking about it reminded me of how much I used to shut down emotionally. I'm still so used to not expressing myself, just not engaging. I just shut down and accommodate, and it's not good for me. I'm just the guy who makes it all okay; I cut people way too much slack.

My sister and her husband are really good about establishing boundaries, and I could learn from them. My father built some stairs for their house, and of course he blew up at some point. So the next time they were doing some house project that he could have helped them with, they just said, "No, we're not going to put ourselves in that situation with him again." My parents were offended, but it was the right thing to do.

How else do you think it's affected you?

I've been pretty upset over having to end a three-year relationship, and I've really wondered, what did I learn from my parents about relationships? I know I wouldn't want to do it the way they did, and I said to my girlfriend way before we broke up, "The difference between our relationship and our parents' is, they value the tangible benefits of marriage. They're enmeshed, they own the house together, and they have this established life. But I've seen what that looks like and I'm telling you right now, even if we had a house and had cars and all of that, I value the emotional connection above all that. I would never want to stay in a relationship that wasn't emotionally satisfying to me."

But we were together for three years and we still couldn't make it work. So that feels like a failure to me. I don't know if relationships can really last, or if they can be good over the long haul. I'm very cynical, and when

I see my friends getting married I'm thinking, "Well, good luck. Let's see how it goes." I think back to when I was seven or eight—I used to think, "When I grow up and get married, I'm going to have one side of the house and she can have the other side so she can't stab me in the back and take all my money." Now that's a strange thought for a kid, but I must have learned it from my father because that's how he acted toward everyone.

The thing for me is to be able to express myself and talk things out even if it means arguing and having to be clear about my own boundaries. That's the hard part for me. I have to learn it from square one.

I can't evaluate in my own head what's fair and what's not fair. Just being accommodating is so easy to fall into. People gravitate to me because I'm so easy to work with, and I kind of like that part of it.

That's the payoff for being so accommodating. Everybody likes you; you're such a mellow guy—
Meanwhile, my sanity is going!

Have you been afraid of becoming like your father?
Definitely. It's been hard for me to learn that it's okay to just be angry. It doesn't mean I'm going to be like him. Anger used to terrify me because I saw it be so out of control for him and I didn't know how to handle it. I used to think it's just a useless emotion because it only hurts people.

What would have made it better for you, growing up?
I think if he had acknowledged that he had some problems and had gotten help for them. He always apologizes after the fact, but nothing ever changes. I don't think he knows how to do things any differently and he never tried to learn how.

How has it been to talk with me about all this?
It's been good. Most people get weirded out if you talk about stuff like this. They think I'm being hard on him or something. I have to explain that I know he's not a bad person, but I do have a right to be angry with him.

I hadn't realized what you said, that he's not trying to intimidate me or be domineering exactly—he's just so driven by his anxiety or whatever it is that he can't control himself. Things upset him, but he's not being a bully.

I'd rather have *him* for a father than my grandfather, that's for sure. I realize that he does want a connection. He's really not trying to cause me harm even though he has screwed things up for me in a lot of ways. I do realize that people aren't just black and white. And I really do appreciate that he has provided for me financially, in terms of tangible things.

But I've also come to accept the fact that he cannot really make an emotional connection with me.

ABOUT BRIAN: MY REFLECTIONS

Brian has recently been in therapy and is discovering more about himself, his family, and the coping strategies he learned in childhood. Because he's a younger sibling, he was spared some of his father's anger, and he could also observe that neither his brother's protests nor his sister's tears helped the situation. He chose the path of appearing to have no reactions or feelings, but as an adult he's finding out the limitations of those choices. He accommodated both to his father and to his mother, and finds himself overaccommodating now in friendships and romantic relationships.

Brian has a good relationship with his mother, yet he's put his finger on one problem between them. Since she wants to stay in the marriage, it makes sense for her to ask Brian not to confront his father, for her sake. Ideally, she could also acknowledge that to Brian that his feelings and reactions are understandable and legitimate; instead, she implies that his reactions are unreasonable and unfair.

I found it odd that Brian's father's anger wasn't particularly personal. As I said to him in the interview, if his father was trying to browbeat Brian or intimidate him, he never would have tolerated Brian's silence or apparent indifference. It seemed to me that his father tries to manage a lot of anxiety and obsessive thinking by yelling or lashing out, but this is very different from a parent who is attempting to assert his dominance or overpower his children.

Although Brian hadn't seen it in that way before, I think his father's obliviousness has allowed Brian to be openly angry with his father without the complicating factor of feeling humiliated or intimidated by him. Early on, he separated himself from his father and seemed to refuse to feel any "shame by association." He knew that his father had problems, he was able to comment on them with other people inside and outside the family, and he doesn't feel responsible for creating those problems or for fixing them.

Brian and I talked about the possibility that his father may have something like Asperger's along with a lot of anxiety. This made sense to him and would certainly explain some angry explosions as well as fixations on objects (like silverware), social awkwardness, and rigidity in doing certain tasks. It can only be guesswork as he's never sought treatment or been evaluated in an attempt to understand his difficulties.

Brian doesn't seem to blame himself for his father's inability to relate to him emotionally, but that unavailability explains his tendency to lose himself in relationships with older male authority figures. "Father hunger" is a very real feeling among young men who haven't been able to connect with their fathers.

WHAT CAN WE LEARN FROM BRIAN?

Sometimes it's an advantage to be a younger sibling. There's often less of a sense of responsibility for family problems and more vantage points from which to observe others without necessarily being in the middle of the action.

Once again, the resilience strategies of youth need to be reworked in adulthood. Shutting down feelings and retreating into an emotional cave probably served Brian well as a boy, since engaging his father didn't work for either of his siblings and certainly wouldn't have worked for him either. But it doesn't work as a way of being in the world as an adult. Therapy can be very helpful in making a transition from being silent, resentful, and accommodating to being able to stand up for yourself and set reasonable boundaries.

Understanding a parent's motivations and emotional makeup can help tremendously in separating and being able to move more freely in one's own life. It can help the child or adult child distinguish between him or herself and a troubled parent and can also help define what's possible in the parent-child relationship.

8

Robert: "I called them the 'nightly shows'—all violence"

Robert is the youngest of 11 children in a family where hostility, ridicule, and even violence were daily occurrences. His mother absented herself from situations in which her husband was particularly abusive to the children, and the children themselves didn't form much of a bond with each other. Robert witnessed, and tried to forget, his father's sexual abuse of an older sister. In fifth grade, he was sent for counseling by his school, but very unfortunately he was disbelieved and ridiculed by the counselor who might have helped him. Robert has had a tough time in life, and he is still struggling with depression and making sense of his life.

You've said you were the youngest of a big family, with 11 children. Can you tell me something about your family when you were a child?

We lived in a lot of different places, and we weren't exactly poor, but always had a hard time financially. The older kids were out of the house, so there was me and two sisters and my parents and sometimes other random cousins who all lived at the house. My older siblings sometimes seemed like aunts or uncles because of the age difference. My father worked, and my mother worked a lot of hours, and sometimes she worked nights. We kids were left alone a lot.

What's the first time you remember realizing that there was something wrong with your father?

I guess it was when I started going to other kids' homes. I remember noticing that their houses were clean and the people weren't yelling and screaming and that they ate dinner together. And there was sort of a sense of caring. It seemed like most of my friends had parents that cared about them and wanted them. And I never felt that way myself.

I remember when I was very young, I witnessed my father being abusive to my sister in different ways. I could hear him at night. I didn't have words for any of it, but he was just very aggressive and my mother was passive. She would just let anything happen.

There must have been some report made about the abuse, because a child protection agency took my sister away for a year or two. Then she came back, but I think she was removed again later on. I tried to block everything out, and I don't know how long my father abused her.

Out of all of us kids, there've been 9 active addicts. I've had addiction problems myself. I just always knew that there was something wrong with us, and it was very embarrassing. I would never bring friends to my house because I wouldn't want them to see how my father treated us. By the way, I don't like the word "Dad."

Why don't you like that word? What did you call your father?

I think that's a title of respect that you earn. I don't think any of us wanted to call him "Dad" because none of us had that kind of feeling for him. We called him "the old man" and some of the older kids called him "George," which is weird because it wasn't even his name. It was kind of a title of disrespect.

What was your father like?

My father could do just about anything. He worked with his hands and he could build things. He could make things happen. He was a take-charge kind of person, and in some ways I'm a lot like him. But he was a rageaholic and he had these really bad mood swings. It was very extreme. He would go from being in a high mood, then the next thing would be verbal abuse, and then he'd be throwing you against the wall and breaking your nose. During the day he seemed pretty normal. He could be polite and friendly and just a regular guy. At night, he would just be a different person.

We had a "nightly show," as I call it, when my father would just tear people apart. We would all sit in the living room where we would watch TV and he would sit on this green half couch that was like his throne. This would be after dinner, which was mostly just "fend for yourself."

At this "nightly show" we knew we had to go and find our seats and just sit there and wait. Once in a great while we would just watch a TV show, but most of the time, all of a sudden, my father would start up. He would start complaining and picking on someone, then he would be yelling and screaming, and a lot of times he would get up and just punch somebody or kick them with no warning.

One particular time, I was about 10 and I must have said something my father didn't like, and he grabbed me by the shirt and slammed me up against the wall. He broke my nose and my collarbone and also my pinky finger. I went to school the next day with my nose taped up with bandages, with two black eyes, and my arm in a sling. Somebody asked me what happened and I said I fell down. Today they would call family services, but then they didn't really question it.

My older sisters and brothers had gone through this school system, so I think the teachers and the administration realized what was going on in my house and they were accustomed to it. At that time your parents were gods and you didn't really question what they did. And the schools didn't really question it either.

Then he did this other thing I just hated. He would talk about what he should've done or what he could've done. He had all these regrets, but he wasn't sad—he was angry. Like for example, we had scrapped an old truck that had been laying around in the yard for years. It was a wreck and it didn't run. Now 20 years later my father's looking back and ranting and raving that "we should've kept that truck. I could've made it run. I should've painted it; I never should have given it away"—and just on and on like that. It wasn't even anything important.

It does sound like time spent in hell. How did you cope with what was happening?

I would try to lose myself in TV programs, or read, or just get away from the house. But there were times I just couldn't take it. The first time I tried to kill myself I was eight or nine. I took a bottle of Nytol. I remember the ads on TV that showed the *N* sideways like a *Z* because it could make you fall asleep. So I took a whole bottle of them, and then I ended up waking up the next morning and I was really disappointed.

What had happened that made things so unbearable right then?

My father had told me to clean my room and I didn't do it. So he kicked out the window and threw out everything in the room. The dresser, the drawers, all my clothes, and all my other stuff including books and toys or whatever. He just threw everything I had out the window. After he did that, I just didn't want to be here anymore.

Did anybody know you took the pills?

No, I didn't say anything. What was the point? It didn't work.

That's a lot of really violent destructive anger coming at you.

There was a lot of verbal abuse too, when he would make fun of all of us kids. I wore glasses and he would call me the professor in this nasty tone of voice. I had some nervous habits like playing with my hair and he would mock me for that. You just ended up assuming that you looked stupid and that you're never going to amount to anything. It's really hard to describe.

I don't know what was worse, the verbal or the physical. He was so explosive, and he could just grab you and beat the hell out of you out of nowhere. He threatened to kill me a few times and he had a gun to back it up. And no subject was off-limits. He would talk about how lousy the sex was with my mother and he would also talk about sexual things he had done with other women.

When he was focused on one of you at these "nightly shows," what would the rest of you do? Where was your mother at those times?

Some nights everybody would get a little bit and then other nights there was a specific target. But if you tried to leave, he would really go bonkers, so we were pretty much trapped.

My mother would sit in the corner of the couch and read a book and act like nothing was happening. I remember many times when my father would hit or kick one of us kids and we would be crying or yelling, and when things got too noisy she would just take the book and go in her room and read there.

I remember a lot of TV shows from back then, and I would try to just go into those TV shows and imagine I was there. The people on the TV were caring and safe and nice, and I wanted to be there instead of where I was.

What were things like when you got to be a little bit older and a little bit more independent, say 9 or 10 years old? Did you have a chance to get away from home more at that point?

In the summertime we would have a bowl of cereal in the morning and then go out all day and not come home till dark. You just wanted to be away as much as you possibly could. I was learning things at home that no kid should be learning.

Did you have other kids that you would consider real friends?

It was more of a pack mentality. Sometimes we just hung out, and at one point I had a newspaper route. A lot of us did odd jobs or various things to make some money. We didn't really talk much to each other, or I didn't anyway; they were just kids to hang out with.

Was that good for you, to have ways to make money?

I didn't really do it to feel good about myself. I just had to do something to get out of there. If I couldn't get out of the house, I would read or watch TV, and I imagined myself in different situations. I guess it was like kids who grew up in war zones—if that's all you know, it's all you know. It just seems normal. Doing other things just helped the time pass.

Actually, there was one thing I liked and that was the Boy Scouts. I liked camping with the Scouts because there were things we had to do, and we learned how to build fires and how to do things. I liked being part of a team. I had a really great Scoutmaster who would help out the kids who didn't have so much money—like he would recycle old Scout uniforms so that we could wear them, things like that. I remember when I got a uniform, and I remember sewing my patches on and feeling really proud of being a Scout. If a kid wanted to go on a camping trip and didn't have the money to pay for the food, the Scoutmaster would make sure it worked out. He was a really great guy. But I have to say, I still felt kind of apart from other people; I still felt like I wasn't as good as they were. Of course I still feel that to this day.

I had a friend that lived a few blocks away and he had the classic *Leave It to Beaver* kind of family. I had dinner at his house sometimes, and it was pretty different because before they would eat they would say grace and sometimes they took me to church on Sunday. I remember thinking, "A family that goes to church together—that's pretty weird." And they would sit down together for a meal and just talk and have a regular conversation. It was like being in a foreign country.

Was there ever a feeling that you could change your own life in some way?

Not really. I look back and I think I was in survival mode. I liked the times I wasn't at home, but I couldn't stay there—it was just a brief break. I didn't see any other kind of a life that I personally could actually have. I never thought it was for me. I just noticed that other people had it.

When I was a little kid I used to wish that the doorbell would ring and somebody would come in and say to my mother, "Your children were switched at birth; these kids have a different mother." But it didn't happen. I was there, it happened, and you can't trade it in.

Apart from the "nightly shows," what was life like at home?

When I was in sixth and seventh grade I would come home from school and clean and make the beds, and sometimes I would make dinner. I was probably trying to make my mom's life easier, but I was also trying to make my life easier. On Sundays, I would make the pasta and sauce my father wanted because it was the only time we had a meal together, and my mother would be tired from working so many hours.

Did you ever have any good times with your father?

I can remember very few good times, mostly when we would be repairing things around the house. I was a lot like him in being very handy and not afraid to try out tools and try fixing things. We could usually work together without his getting angry.

What was your relationship like with your mother during all this time?

I always thought I really loved my mother a lot, but I've come to realize lately that we had a kind of a strange relationship. Sometimes she would say that she loved me or she loved us kids, but I realize that a lot of the time I just felt like I was in her way. Because if it wasn't for me coming along as the youngest, she would've been out of there a lot sooner. She never said that out loud, but it was a kind of feeling that I always had.

Sometimes my mother would try to get away from my father, so she would just run away. She would throw some clothes in the car and put us in the car and just take off. It happened a few times and it would usually end up being about the length of the school year. The first time I remember I was really pretty young and we went to a place in upstate New York. The only things in the town were an eyeglass factory, a post office, and a general store, and you got the school bus at 6 a.m. I don't know why she picked that place. Maybe she knew someone there, but to me it just seemed like it was some random place that was far enough away from my father. But somehow my father found us and we went back.

In some ways it was really good to be away from my father, but in another way for a young kid it was just incredibly boring. My mother got a job in this eyeglass factory so she worked a lot of hours, and at night sometimes she would get drunk. The school was awful for me because it was in the middle of nowhere and it was very strict, and I ended up on the receiving end of the principal's belt more than once.

So that year didn't seem to be a significant break for you emotionally?

I didn't think of it that way. It just seemed to be a matter of time before we went back. It didn't seem like we were building some new life that was going to be different.

The last time she left was just when I turned 16, and I'm the youngest. She went to live with her mother after her father died, and I quit school and started living in my car until I could get a job and earn some money to live on. It felt like she just abandoned me, but I also felt guilty because maybe she could have left him earlier if I hadn't been around. She didn't go back to him this last time.

She let a lot of things happen to a lot of us, and the whole lot of us are very screwed up. I mean, I've been divorced two times and I don't have a brother or sister who hasn't been in screwed-up relationships. We're all broken in one way or another.

Did you ever talk to her about any of this, either at the time or later on when you were an adult?

When I got a little older there were times that she and I would talk, and I guess maybe there was some kind of closeness there. But I still struggle a lot with the fact that she let so much bad stuff happen to us. I just really can't come to terms with that. Later on she said to me, "I had nowhere to go, and I always had kids. It wasn't like today." I don't really buy it.

Do you remember anyone at school being concerned about what was happening to you at home? Or was there any concern about your behavior at school?

The school made me go to a psychologist or a counselor or somebody when I was in fifth grade. They set it up for one year, and the school would transport three or four of us to this place every week, which must have been some kind of a clinic. I also went all through one summer. I didn't want to go and I didn't talk for a while, but he kept probing me. So I finally got to the point of thinking, "Okay, so you want to know what's going on? Here's what's going on." So I told him. I sat there and I told him things that I never told anyone before. I told him what was going on with the nightly shows, and I told him about some stuff one of my brothers was doing to me. And I told him about my father and my sister. All of it.

Did that take a lot of courage on your part? Did you feel like you could trust this guy?

I think it was more just kind of "Screw it." Then, at some point he told me it would be the last time I would be talking to him. I don't know if the money ran out or what.

So this last time, he said, "So let's trade places for a minute." So we switched chairs and he sat like I would sit, with my leg over the arm of the chair, and he said to me, "Now I'm going to be telling you the biggest lies and the tallest stories you've ever heard," and he just started mocking me for all the things I had told him. On the outside I was laughing at him, but on the inside it was horrible. He told me he thought I was the biggest storyteller that he had ever heard and that I was a liar. I wish I were kidding about this, but I'm not. I can still see his face and I can remember exactly what his office looked like.

This is a horrible breach of trust from somebody in his position. What was your reaction?

I decided that people like you [gesturing to me] are basically full of shit and you have to just tell them what they want to hear. It sure kept me from trusting anybody for a long time.

Did you and your brothers and sisters ever talk to each other about what was going on?

We would mock my father and imitate him, obviously when he wasn't there. We would use different funny voices and say stuff like, "Get in the house right now, goddamn it, and when I get my hands on you I'm going to break your neck." Any humor in our family was always at someone's expense, like teasing people about things that they were really self-conscious about. That's kind of what we thought of as relaxation. Just teasing each other in a mean way until people's feelings were hurt.

So it doesn't sound like there was any sense of sibling solidarity, any kind of emotional alliance.

No, it was survival of the fittest. We still to this day don't have that bond. My brother was in trouble a lot, and I would buy him some stuff and send him packages when he was in juvie [juvenile detention]. But now he won't return a phone call. We live an hour away from each other, but we only see each other a couple of times a year and have lunch. But we don't really connect.

The point was to get through life one day at a time. I really thought I wasn't going to make it to 50 because my father always told me he was going to kill me. He would put a gun to my head and click the trigger. It was absolutely insane. I don't want to give him any excuse for what he did, but he has to have been insane. It's absolutely amazing that nobody got seriously hurt or killed. I remember the day we put him in the nursing home with Alzheimer's, he told me, "Before I go to the old folk's home I'm going to kill you; I'm going to put a bullet in you." This was after I took care of him at home when he couldn't care for himself.

That's pretty crazy behavior, and it must have been terrifying for you.

There were guns in the house growing up and my father carried guns in his car. I thought about using one on him on a number of occasions. Once when I was a teenager my mother opened the window and pointed a shotgun at my father. She pulled the trigger and nothing happened, so she pulled it again. I guess it was empty. I still remember the clicks. He and I were outside and I think if the gun had been loaded, it would have ended up hitting me too.

I wanted this miracle to happen; in my fantasies I had the perfect life, with a family that loved me and wanted me. I've felt many times, life is just not worth living. I know there were some people that probably cared about me, but nobody cared enough to try to help me. One of my older brothers could have done something, or tried to get us younger kids out of the house, but it never happened. A lot of people who should have been paying attention have closed their eyes to my circumstances. I always just fell through the cracks. And the one time I did tell somebody the truth of what was happening, it was a disaster. So why bother? What's the point?

Those feelings are so strong as you're talking about it. It's still really painful to think of.

The thing I learned growing up is that you have to hurt people before they have an opportunity to hurt you. That makes you a respected force. It's taken me a long time to unlearn that. I've had a good therapist the last couple of years, otherwise I would probably be a train wreck. I'm doing this [the interview] so hopefully I can help someone else.

My therapist is really the only one that understands me. It's kind of scary because nobody has ever taken the time or cared enough to actually try and understand me. I started out thinking that maybe I would see her for six or eight weeks, and it's probably been two or three years at this point.

* * *

What reactions did you have after our first interview?

I was pretty bummed out for about a week. Unfortunately, it brought up some memories I hadn't really thought of before, and I don't want to get into it, but I'll just say there was way too much sexual stuff going on with kids when I was growing up. I talked to my therapist about it.

Okay. Are you okay to talk some more today? I know these interviews can be tough.

No, I'm okay. The part I feel good about is that this might help somebody else. I've done some good things and I've done some bad things in my life, and it feels good to do something positive like this. But it's not easy.

I have a lot of respect for you for coming back for the second interview. So, just to catch up with where we left off, I hadn't asked about any extended family that might have been involved when you were growing up.

The only extended family would be my grandmother, my mother's mother. She was pretty much of a bitch, and whatever you did it was never good enough. I could've discovered the cure for leukemia or landed on the moon, and it wouldn't have been good enough for her. Anything that my father had anything at all to do with was no good, because she had been against my mother marrying my father in the first place.

I remember telling her once about something I learned in school and she just said to me, "Oh, you're so stupid. That's all wrong. I can't believe you're so dumb." Or I would try to do my math homework, which I had trouble with, and she would just say, "I can't believe how stupid you are. It's because your mother married that idiot of a father. She used to be such a pretty girl and now look at her."

How were you doing with school at that point?

I'm a pretty capable person, but I never did well in school. If I came home and put my schoolbooks on the kitchen table where my father could see them, he would go off. My mother didn't do much to help. She would sometimes correct me if I read something wrong, like a sign or bumper sticker, but her tone was more like, "What are you, stupid?"

Did you keep your home life and your other activities separate from each other?

Oh yes, absolutely. Especially after I had that bad experience with the counselor, I really didn't trust anybody. I never talked about what went on at home. I didn't really talk to anybody about anything. I just thought the people in authority were basically kind of full of it, and the idea is you just go through life and there are some things you just don't talk about. Sometimes another kid might say his dad hit him or belted him, but I knew the level of violence that we had in my home was not common at all.

What were you learning about being a man?

I definitely didn't want to be like my father. But when I was a kid I was learning how to survive, how to be a scrapper, how to lie, how to be violent, all that. In my family if someone accused you of something, the proper reaction was to go from zero to anger in half a second. If you didn't, that was an admission of guilt.

In junior high school, things started to get harder. That was the first time I couldn't just to do my homework on the school bus. I had to lay my books out on a table; I had to do research; I had to write papers and do book reports. That's when I realized what a poor student I was. I missed a lot of school days, but nobody seemed to notice or even mind. It seems like they just expected it.

How were you relating to your father at that time, as you got to be an older teenager?

At a certain point I got bigger and stronger and I became a challenge to him. When I got to be stronger, I stood up to him for the first time instead of running and cowering. That was the beginning of the change when he realized he couldn't beat me up anymore.

I also realized that, like my father, I had a talent for fixing things and using tools. I could have benefited from some guidance right then because I had a good science teacher in ninth grade and I started to get A's for the first time. I really liked it and I would see other kids doing science projects, but it seemed complicated and I had no idea how to go about doing something like that. I think if I had gotten a little more support from school right then, I might have felt a little better. But it's hard to know because after that year I think I was also starting to hate myself. I hated what I was becoming. I hated where I lived and how I lived. Then when I turned 16, my mother left for good and I had to drop out. I've gone back since then, but that was the end of any chance of getting help at school.

It was around this time that I joined a church and got into fundamentalist religion. I somehow was hoping that there would be a lightning strike and everything would be made okay, that I would somehow be healed of everything that I carried with me and healed of all the things I had done. Everything would be okay.

I got involved with a woman there, the mother of my son, and we ended up getting married, even though we shouldn't have. I was really deeply into this church and I was ordained a minister there when I was about 20. But I couldn't handle any of it. I had a lot of trouble with my temper at home, then I got started with alcohol, and the church meanwhile was teaching me that women are supposed to be subservient to men. I liked that, being in charge of somebody for once.

Long story short, I ended up being asked to leave that church, and all the people who had been my "friends" there suddenly wouldn't talk to me. I had screwed things up royally, but I couldn't take being shunned like that. I decided it wasn't worth going on and I drove my car into a tree going about 80, but it totaled the car and I survived. I felt like I couldn't even commit suicide right, and this was the second time I had tried.

My marriage fell apart; I was still drinking; I carried a gun; I was living different places and trying to work and make enough money to pay my bills. But I was just so angry with everyone and everything. I thought

I was supposed to arrive at a point where I would have this perfect life. But it always turned out that it was just *me* after all.

And at this point I ended up back with my father. He was sick and alone because not one of his kids wanted to have anything to do with him. He got very ill and I ended up taking total care of him: bathing him, feeding him. He was still a bastard. He got mad and told me to leave, and then he got enraged with me that I left him alone. He eventually was diagnosed with Alzheimer's and went to a nursing home.

Meanwhile, I had another really bad relationship with a woman who was very crazy. We got married and had a little girl, who was the most beautiful little being I had ever seen, and she only lived for three days. I didn't know how to deal with it.

I was angry and belligerent all time and I was still carrying a gun. I ended up threatening some guy with it, and I held the gun right up to his head. I think I came really close to just impulsively killing the guy. I ended up serving three years in jail.

In jail I met this guy who was kind of a counselor and a minister. He had grown up in a home for fatherless boys so we kind of connected. I talked to him a lot, not so much about my family, but just what was going on with me and how confused and angry I was. He gave me books to read, and he gave me some good advice and I started to get my head together.

When I got out, I started to do better. I have a decent job now and I'm trying to help my son out. My wife now is pretty disabled and I take of her too. My parents are gone, and the sister that I was closest to, the one my father messed with, ended up committing suicide a few years ago. Maybe it was financial problems, maybe other stuff, I don't know.

What are some of the things you continue to have a hard time with now?

I find as I get older that I'm getting more like my father and it's scary. I don't want to be thought of as "the old man." I'd like to be thought of with love and affection. I can be standing somewhere and I suddenly realize I'm standing just like he did. I don't want to do that. I don't want any of his mannerisms and I don't want any of his habits.

I still take meds for depression and I still feel suicidal at times. I've talked about it with my therapist. There's just a lot to try to come to terms with. I don't feel like a victim of my childhood, but I do feel I learned so many wrong things and I haven't always been so great myself. I kind of wish I could forgive more, but then I think, I can't really do that yet. I still feel like it's letting people off the hook and it doesn't seem right.

I sometimes feel like I'm very toxic and that I don't deserve to be loved or cared for. I've struggled with those feelings for a long time. Sometimes my therapist will say caring things to me and they're nice to hear, but it's a little bit late in the game. She says it's important to admit that I was victimized, which is a step, but I don't like to think of myself as a victim. That's an excuse and a crutch and it's a form of weakness.

I still have my demons and my nightmares at night, and even sitting here I'm remembering stuff. Sometimes I still hope it's all a bad dream. I keep hoping that these are all "false memories" and I really had a wonderful childhood.

What do you think would have helped back when you were growing up?

The biggest thing would have been to stop my father from being so violent. If someone had been able to do something about that, not just let it go on and on. I know my mother felt bad about it, but she just walked away too. I know she was a victim, but I still feel she had a few options too. Because that stuff just shouldn't have happened.

I guess the best I could say is, I'm not responsible for what happened to me, but I'm responsible for not carrying it on.

ABOUT ROBERT: MY REFLECTIONS

Robert's story is daunting. The damage from his father's relentless emotional and physical violence has been very hard for him to overcome, and he continues to struggle with it. His mother's apparent indifference is chilling. I think there may have been some early maternal care though, since Robert felt as a child that they had a close relationship. He didn't depict her as a neglectful or indifferent mother before these "nightly shows," as he calls them. He's ambivalent about forgiving her; at least his mother tried to explain her actions, thus acknowledging that there was some failure on her part. He sees her, correctly I think, as a beaten-down, depressed, overwhelmed mother with few resources, and not as someone who hated him or deliberately hurt or neglected him.

It's difficult to disagree with his assessment of his father as a sadistic and cruel man, although there must be some history there to make sense of it. He may well have been bipolar; the "manic" swing in bipolar disorder sometimes manifests itself as rage and explosiveness rather than euphoria and grandiosity. This degree of sustained violence is often linked to alcohol or drug abuse, but not for Robert's father.

A strong sibling alliance can be a buffering force in some families like this, but unfortunately Robert and his siblings were alienated and hostile to each other. Possibly the age range was such that there just wasn't enough cohesion to help these kids bond well to each other; on the other hand, in some families with an age spread, the older siblings care for the younger ones in times of trouble.

In a story like this, where the family is so lacking in support, it's especially outrageous to hear of a child trusting someone outside the family and finding only ridicule and disbelief. Robert's counselor had a chance to be supportive and encouraging at the very least, and instead he made Robert's situation incalculably worse. If he didn't believe Robert's stories, he could have checked out the facts through school records or by asking someone who knew the family. Instead, he ridiculed Robert after months of supposedly sympathetic listening. What little trust might have been built was completely shattered, not only with that particular person but also with any one of "you people" long into the future.

Had the counselor been even minimally competent, he could have protected Robert from some of the worst effects of the earlier damage. Had Robert been told the obvious—that he was not the cause of his father's wrath, and that his father had problems beyond what Robert could see— it would have diminished some of the feeling of "badness" that he carries to this very day.

From that point on, Robert was on a downward trajectory. He felt he had been abandoned by his mother and began to abuse drugs and alcohol; he had trouble coping with feelings of intense anger and desperation. He wanted to find something good and hopeful, but undermined his own efforts at every turn. All of this points not only to his early childhood experience but also to the lack of help along the way.

On a hopeful note, however, he was still remarkably open to good influences that came his way. In prison, he did connect with a mentor of sorts. He did try to turn things around even as he repeated some of the old patterns.

At this point in his life, he is still struggling with depression, guilt, and anger, with what his life means and what good and what harm he's done. He's still seeking and still trying to make sense of things. I was impressed and moved that he agreed to be interviewed for the book and that he knew his story was worth telling. As he himself pointed out to me, a few years ago he wouldn't have done so. His current therapist may be "too late" for some things, but he has stuck with her and is still listening.

Robert's own native intelligence and his ability to remain open despite all that's happened to him are strong resilient features in his makeup. But because there was so much damage done early, and so little done along the way to help him, he has lived many years with a belief in his own badness. For him, being heard and believed may be important steps on a path to healing.

WHAT CAN WE LEARN FROM ROBERT'S STORY?

Sadly, what we can learn is that almost everything that happened to Robert made matters worse, not better. There doesn't seem to be any single person who reassured, comforted, or stood up for Robert, nor anyone to assure him that he didn't cause and wasn't responsible for his father's treatment of him.

When children are told, repeatedly, that they are "bad," they will internalize a core sense of badness that is very difficult to reach back and undo. This is why early intervention and protection are so important. Even if a child has to stay in a destructive environment, just knowing that there's someone who doesn't see him as bad can be somewhat protective. It's especially important where a parent is directly hostile, aggressive, and verbally abusive to a child. A schizophrenic father who's hallucinating is less damaging to a child's sense of self than a nonpsychotic parent who is specifically targeting the child for name-calling, humiliation, and belittling.

Resilience can appear where one least expects it, and Robert's story reminds us to be open-minded and willing to be surprised. I believed Robert when he told me that a few years ago he wouldn't have set foot in my office, thinking "those people are all full of shit." The surprise is, given all he's been through, that he's still trying and still taking risks in an effort to find some peace and contentment.

9

Tim: "Mom painted her bedroom midnight blue"

Tim is the middle of three children, having an older brother and a younger sister. He grew up in the New England area and the family moved many times. His parents divorced when Tim was 11, and his father went to the West Coast where he maintained only occasional contact with the kids. Tim's mother had short periods of being "up" but was depressed for years, leaving the kids to their own devices. Tim tried to help but was berated by his mother for not loving her enough. He's now self-employed and lives with a longtime girlfriend, and he explores various avenues to help himself as he still struggles with depression.

What's your first memory of something being "off" with your mother?

Nothing specific, but I was about eight years old when I just had a feeling that things weren't right with the family, things weren't right with Mom. There had been ups and downs before, and my parents fought all the time, but something seemed worse when I was about eight.

What did you notice?

I know she was hospitalized when I was 10, but what I remember was just a feeling of it being an empty home. My father traveled a lot. I can clearly picture the neighborhood and my school, but I can't picture either one of my parents. It's like I don't want to remember the house or my mother or father.

You moved a lot, yes?

We moved every year or two. One year especially Mom seemed warmer with us, and I remember how happy she was about her artwork, going shopping for arts and crafts things, buying antiques, and hanging around with other artists. That was a good year. That was actually the best year we ever had, when I was around seven or eight.

What happened after that year?

We moved again and I just have this overall vague memory of everything being kind of empty again. Then when I was about 10, she went into the hospital. My father was still living with us then.

What do you remember about that? Did anyone explain it to you?

I remember the letters YPI [Yale Psychiatric Institute] so I know she was at Yale. But nobody sat us down to talk about what was going on. There was a visiting room on the second or third floor, and we would go in there to see her. I think she was maybe wearing a nightgown. I didn't know what to say to her. What does a 9- or 10-year-old kid know about talking to a parent who's in the mental hospital? I remember just standing around not knowing what to do, and my brother and sister the same thing. We were supposed to go up and kiss her and stuff, but it just felt off.

Is there anything else you remember about that time she was in the hospital?

My father had to be around more and be the parent. He had to cook, which he never did before. When she came home I remember her cooking a lot less because we all had learned to cook certain things and we had all learned about TV dinners. I did more of that than my brother or sister. I would make lunch and I would try to make meals, and I would try to pick up the house a little bit.

She wouldn't be up in the morning when we went to school. She would be there when we got home, but not doing anything, maybe just in her room in her nightgown.

I still to this day creep around my own house—it's so embarrassing to admit this, but it's true! And my brother and sister did it all the time when we were younger. We'd creep around like we didn't want to be caught. My girlfriend and I live together, but we each have our own room. I absolutely hate for her to call me into her room. 'Cause when I was little, if you made any noise, my mom might yell at you for that, or she might call you and tell you to come in her room, and then she wanted you to give her a backrub. It was creepy and we all would just be as quiet as we could because we never wanted to hear her voice. We would have to give her a neck massage or a back massage with cocoa butter. I don't remember anything sexual, but it was always dark in there. Toward the end of her life she painted her bedroom midnight blue. My sister said, "Who the fuck does that kind of thing?"

You and your siblings all felt pretty much the same about it? That it was unpleasant? Not that it was a time to be with Mom or hang out with her?

No, it was something to avoid. I just have a persistent dread of any situation like that. I know it's affected me a lot, because when I've had girlfriends, if they get sick and need me to take care of them, I just feel awful and I can't do it. Oddly enough, I like taking care of people generally, but that particular scenario just creeps me out.

My sister ended up running away from home at 14 and she was found living in California. So she had to come home. But I think we kind of envied her. Then my mom got remarried and my sister was the only one left at home. She used to call that time "the cocoa-butter years."

Where was your father during these earlier years?

He got up early and went to work, and then he'd come home late and drink. I don't remember much about him. He didn't ever have much to do with us, really.

My mom waited till he was traveling, which he did a lot, and she sat us down and explained that they were going to get a divorce. I think we kind of knew it was coming, because he was never home anyway and they argued and fought a lot when he was home. She told us we had a choice. We could either stay with her or go with my father, but he was going to be living in California.

That was really a heavy decision. I remember a lot of guilt about that one. I really wanted to go with my father, but I knew she wanted us to stay with her. There was this underlying threat that she wouldn't survive if we left, and if we left, it would be like divorcing her. We all chose to stay with her. I still regret that because I could have gone to a good school where my father was, and I could have had a relationship with him and things might have worked out better. It was kind of like hearing the prison door close with you on the wrong side.

So there was an implicit threat that she would—what?—commit suicide?

Yeah, she had said other times when she was depressed that she was going to kill herself, so I don't remember if she said it right then, but it was definitely implied. You definitely knew if you wanted to leave, there was going to be something that happened and it wouldn't be good.

That's a pretty huge and unfair responsibility to hang on you as a kid and on your siblings.

Well, the weird thing is, after the divorce it didn't seem to matter that we had decided to stay with her. She got much worse and kept accusing us of not loving her. She would wake us all in the middle of the night, and she'd make us all come downstairs in our pajamas. We would barely be awake. She'd get us all to sit at the kitchen table and then it would start, and it could on for a few hours, in the middle of the night. She would cry hysterically or yell at us, and she just kept repeating things like, "Why are you doing this to me? Why don't you love me?" And she would aim this mostly at me, according to my sister. I've kind of blocked out the details.

We would make some kind of phony confession, like, "We're sorry, we love you," and then she might stop. Otherwise we would just sit there and wait for her to be finished. If she had been a drinker, it would be easier to understand, but she was completely sober when she went on these rants.

How did your brother and sister react?

At those times? We just sat there and when she was through we just went back to bed. We didn't talk about it except to maybe make some crack here or there. Otherwise my brother stayed away from the house as much as he could, and my sister like I said ran away for a while. I guess I took the most care of her.

Were there any other adults—relatives, teachers, neighbors—anyone else who took any interest or might have known things weren't so good at your house?

We had moved every few years so we didn't really have any connections like that. My parents didn't have friends, really. We were kind of isolated from other people I guess. Nothing ever felt like it was going to last very long.

Seems like it's hard to remember these years very well, like it drains your energy to even think about it. Is that how it feels to talk about it?

Definitely. It's kind of foggy—not like I can't remember but more like it's all shrouded in fog. Maybe that's how it felt to me at the time. It was always just a heavy kind of feeling in the house. I have the feeling I just don't want to remember a lot of stuff from back then. Not like it's some kind of repressed memory or anything, but it's so empty . . .

How did you cope?

I liked reading comics, and I had a very active fantasy life. I had this fantasy for a very long time of rescuing women, especially rescuing very tiny women. Tinkerbelle was my "baby." From the time I was 10, 11, 12— I always liked the idea of very tiny women that I could hold in my hand.

They seemed safe and they seemed like they were right there, that they liked me, that they would spend time with me.

We had hundreds of comics, and we also had things we could build. In the summer my brother and I would roam around outside even at night. Nobody cared. I did have friends whose houses I would go to, and I remember they liked me, but I never felt like I fit in anywhere. Just not fitting in, that's how I perceive myself. Like right now, people know me and are friendly to me in the whole neighborhood where I live, but I feel like I don't belong.

How was school going for you during this time?

I liked to sing and my teacher had me sing once in front of a whole group of kids. She told me to sing some song that I hated, and I botched it up and all the kids laughed. My teacher laughed too and said, "That's terrible." From then on I've had this fear that groups are going to laugh at me, so that doesn't help.

It also doesn't help that I've always been small. I didn't usually get picked for sports things, even though I could do a lot of push-ups and I was pretty strong for my size.

Were there any other people to help you out—any men or older boys, for example?

Really, nobody. My older brother wasn't interested; in fact, my brother picked on me physically a lot and my mother didn't stop him. And by this time my father was gone. I wasn't in Scouts or anything like that.

My brother wouldn't beat up on me, but he might kind of bully me if he wanted something. I was told I had a very bad temper when I was younger, and I took karate lessons, which I really enjoyed. Then, my brother was giving me a hard time and I got into a karate stance and that was the end of the karate lessons. My mother made me stop. She didn't want my brother to get hurt.

She said I wasn't allowed to use karate on him—so what was the point if he was six inches taller and 40 pounds heavier than me? I felt really angry about that because it was the one chance I had to fight back, but she decided to protect him instead of me.

Did your mother ever pay attention to you in a good way, that you remember, or give you advice or guidance?

Once in a while, but no warm fuzzies. Once she told me it was okay to punch a kid in the face who was tormenting me, and because it was so rare to get her attention, I listened to her. It didn't work out all that well in the end, but I did punch the kid and that was probably a good thing.

When I was younger she was more involved and more helpful; she would help with homework or come into the school to do something. I remember her being a better mom during that one year, where she was so happy and she just paid a lot more attention and we had like a normal family.

It sounds like you, and your brother too, felt very disconnected from any adults, including your mother, and didn't really have many other connections either.

That pretty much describes it. After a couple of years though, my mother seemed to be feeling better, the kitchen table talks stopped for a while, and she was dating. So she got remarried to this guy and he was an okay guy, but he didn't have a lot to do with us because he had two kids of his own.

We moved yet again, but by that time I was feeling pretty depressed and confused. Then after a while she and the new husband started fighting all the time, and the same old stuff was going on. She'd get angry with everyone, including me, for just anything at all.

Did she ever see a therapist, was she in treatment at all, or did she take medication?

She was always seeing some psychiatrist or other, but my sister and I used to joke that she couldn't be telling them everything. My sister used to say, "She can't be telling them what a bitch she is." She took meds, I don't remember what, but it seemed to be just hit or miss. I didn't pay all that much attention because it didn't seem to make any difference. I think what I heard from somewhere was that she was bipolar, which makes sense.

What was it like when she was remarried?

We liked him okay; but like I said, it's not like he was a role model or anything. We tried to tell him about how she would just stay in her bed or in her room all the time, and how we were afraid she would do something to herself, but he just ignored us and didn't want to hear it. I guess he had to see it for himself. He was there for a few years and I went off to college, then they got divorced. She immediately met another guy and got married a third time.

What was going on with your siblings then?

My brother cut off the whole family a long time ago. I think it was when I was about 30. My mother showed me a letter he wrote. He just said he wasn't part of the family anymore and wasn't going to have anything to do with anyone, period. And nobody's heard from him since then. So that's about 20 years. So I guess it's basically just me and my sister left.

That's pretty final, I guess. You don't know what prompted him to do that?

I have no idea. I hadn't been in contact with him anyway, so it wasn't a big change.

If we go back to when you were an adolescent, what was going on between you and your dad then?

When I was about 15 I went to London and to Paris, and I saw my dad there. By that time he was working in various cities in Europe and I saw him both places. Then my brother and sister and I went to Europe sometime later than that and saw him for a few weeks.

How did you get along with him? What was he like?

He was very aloof. He drank a lot and he was always in a business suit. He was nice enough, but there was no real sharing or opening up or buddy-buddy.

But when we would visit him, or when I did by myself, he worked most of the time, and he would bring work back to his apartment. It's not like he really wanted to get to know us all that well. Once he did bring me some coins because I collected coins and that was pretty nice.

Did he have any interest in life on the home front? Was he concerned about how things were with your mother?

We didn't talk about it. He didn't ask and I certainly wasn't going to say anything. I didn't really feel any closer to him than to anybody else, and I've never talked to people about my family life or how I grew up.

How do you think people would react if you talked to them about it?

I guess I assume people would be disgusted by it. There was so much weird stuff with my mother, and I also felt like I was just a bad kid who was hurting my mother in some way. I assumed people would think the same thing and just be turned off to it. I felt pretty worthless. It's confusing because I tried to help her when I was younger, but at a certain point I just hated her and wanted her to leave me alone. But that just made me feel bad about myself. Just talking about it now makes me feel like it would be embarrassing to talk about it with anybody except a therapist. Who wants to hear this crap?

Did you start to have friends or girlfriends in high school?

I tried to have girlfriends, but I remember my mother never liked them. There was one girl who was really nice, but my mother hated her. That girl, and some other people I knew then, knew about this world of comfort and friendships and relationships, where people liked each other and were comfortable—but I couldn't even really comprehend it.

How were you doing in school then, and what was going on at home?

High school was okay; I could get decent grades. I didn't feel like I fit in, but I did have a few friends. Home was still pretty bad. I think I still needed some parental attention or something, but I think the only times she paid attention to me were when she wanted something from me. I did try to make her feel better; I would try to decorate the house at Christmas, but she always fucked things up. If I tried to make some kind of holiday for the family at home, she wouldn't come out of her room or she would be in a horrible mood or something. There was really no point. When my brother and sister and I would come home for Thanksgiving—this is after we were adults—we would joke around and take bets about whether or not she would even come downstairs.

And if she came downstairs, would she be dressed like a normal person or would she come in her nightgown and start some huge fight? She might attack me or attack my brother. Once I just got so upset, I yelled at her to "just shut up, I'm not going to take this anymore." And she started screaming and saying, "Get out, get out," and I just didn't care anymore. But mostly we never confronted her because we didn't want to see her go bonkers or just be more pitiful and moping around and being depressed.

What was it like when you went off to college? Did she help you at all in leaving home at that point?

She didn't help me. She said she didn't have any money, and she was also having some kind of breakdown when I moved out and went off to college. I got scholarships, and my father also helped me out a little bit financially. One time I came home from college on a break and she got mad I was playing my guitar, and she grabbed it and was going to throw it out the window. My stepfather stopped her. I started smoking dope; I drank a little bit—just trying to escape.

What happened after you went off to college? You didn't go back home to live, I think you've told me.

No. Well, I went back very briefly after I graduated. But then for some reason or other she threw me out when I was 22, no notice, no money, no clothes, no nothing. She might have thrown me out because I was high, because I was high a lot. I ended up getting a room in some factory where the windows were all painted black. Really cheerful.

She had gotten worse and just let herself go to hell. I couldn't really tolerate even seeing her much anymore. She was married to the third husband, but I did hear that they had big fights too and that once she walked to the next town in her nightgown after one of their fights.

Once in a great while I would stop by to see her and she would usually start talking to me and confiding in me about stuff. She told me about my brother basically divorcing the whole family and she showed me the letter he wrote. She bitched a lot about that.

What kind of state was she in then? Were you concerned about her?

Well, I knew there had been suicide attempts in there somewhere, because her husband took her to the ER once and called me. She had taken another overdose. I went over to see her, and she looked terrible. She had been really attractive, but she looked pale and puffy and apathetic, just awful. I saw her a couple more times.

I didn't see her very often because I didn't want to. But my sister went because she had three kids and she thought the kids should know their grandmother. My mother ended up killing herself when I was 35.

I really didn't see that coming, Tim. What happened?

The police came to the school where I was teaching and they just told me, "You need to come down to the station." So I thought, "This can't be good." I went with them and they told me what happened, but they wouldn't let me see her. So I yelled at them, I don't even really remember, and they finally said, "Okay," and so I saw her. (Cries)

[I'm very taken aback by this coming so unexpectedly in the interview and it seems like he's telling me something he himself had forgotten. It seems it happened a few months ago, not 20 years ago.]

She's really gone. Why did she do that? I didn't have any words. My stepfather and I just looked at each other and hugged each other. There's nothing to say. It's inexpressible. She shot herself in the head. You have to put the gun in your mouth so you hit the base of the spinal cord and there's no chance to survive. They had just wrapped up her head and there was a tube in her mouth. She was covered in sheets. That's what I saw. Then I went back to their house and there was blood spattered around and a bullet hole in the ceiling. He had taken the mattress out and put it somewhere else.

Why did she do it? We didn't know. And nobody talked about it because everybody was talking about the will because she had changed the will a few weeks prior. She had cut out us three and left everything to her husband.

My sister's reaction was "The bitch finally did it." I don't even remember what my brother said, but it was suddenly all about the money, little as it was.

It was almost like we were arguing about selling a car or something. There was no funeral. She wanted a cremation and I ended up with the ashes.

What else do you remember about this time? It doesn't sound like there was any family connection—was there anyone else who you could turn to?

Well, it's not something you really want to go around telling people. I was in shock for a long time. I ended up going to this lake that my mother had liked, that we had picnicked on years before. I always remembered it. So I thought I would scatter her ashes there. It didn't really register that now it was on somebody's private property. So this security guy showed up and asked me what was I doing there, and I said, "I'm going to scatter my mom's ashes"—and I guess I was foolishly hoping for some sympathy or understanding or something. So he said, "So in addition to trespassing, you're going to litter, too? I'm calling the cops." So I had to go to the station and I was there for hours, and when I went before the judge he ended up apologizing to me when he heard the whole story.

What impact did your mother's suicide have on you?

I think it's just added to the depression, frankly, and makes me feel even more embarrassed about my family. I don't really talk about it. And I think it's probably why I have suicidal thoughts when I get down.

How have things been for you since that, as an adult?

I've had various jobs including as a teacher, and I've recently been doing some consulting for various businesses. I like it and I'm pretty good at it and I might try starting up my own business at some point. I have a hard time focusing on a goal and pushing through obstacles and that might be partly due to depression—I'm not sure. In my mid-30s, before I was married, I probably drank too much. I was teaching then and I would just come home and drink and be on the computer. I guess I was pretty lost. At one time I was interested in "past lives," but I think I'm having enough trouble with this one for right now, thank you very much! [laughs]

Do you still struggle with depression, then?

Yeah, I guess it's been on and off. I don't like taking medication, so I'm trying to see myself in a better light and realize that people do like me and I am a competent person. Sometimes I feel great; other times if I get really down, I have thoughts about suicide, but I'd never do anything. It's very fleeting.

Have you been in therapy?

I've seen a couple of therapists, but it hasn't really helped. I did the Landmark Forum, which was interesting, but I'm not sure what it really did in the long run.

How has it been in relationships?

I was married for about 10 years. I guess you would call us co-dependent. I always felt trapped, but I was never trapped, really, because we didn't have kids and she wasn't financially dependent on me. But I tend to fall back into codependency and stay in relationships and feel trapped even though I can leave anytime.

Does it feel like how you felt growing up, the trapped feeling?

Well, now that you mention it. There was kind of a similar feeling. I did get divorced, and now I'm living with a woman and I'm not sure where it's going. I think about breaking up, but I'm not sure. She also gets pretty depressed and has horrible self-esteem.

What would have made a difference to you, growing up, Tim? If something could have been different?

If my mother had been nurturing, if she had taken us places and stuff. I was a good little kid; I liked things like cleaning up and cooking. We had that one year, that was all. If she could have stayed like that, I guess. Happy.

I just feel like I have all this horrible stuff inside me, and when I'm there I think I'm pretty bad. But when I'm in a different state of mind, I think I'm okay. When I'm up I'm really okay, but it's hard to stay there. There's stuff that's right below the surface.

ABOUT TIM: MY REFLECTIONS

Tim was given only one role in his family: to be his mother's caretaker. This may have been the only time he truly felt he had a "place" where he belonged. When he was young, the caretaking felt more innocent and genuine to him, as he cooked meals, decorated the Christmas tree, and tried to clean up a bit when his mother was isolated in her bedroom. As he got older, he dreaded being called into her bedroom to sit with her or massage her back, and I believe he has considerable guilt about this change in his attitude. This is the kind of thing that feels like disloyalty to a child.

He doesn't recall any explanations about his mother's moods, withdrawal, or even her hospitalization. Despite his poor memory, it sounds likely that there wasn't much effort made to help these kids cope with their mother.

Tim was aware of how hard it was not to choose his father after the divorce, but his anger was suffused with guilt. In essence, their father was turning over their mother's care to his kids, since he moved far away and had little contact after he left. Some divorced spouses make efforts to be close by, to help their kids, or even try to get custody of the children. Those children usually feel somewhat less abandoned than Tim and his siblings must have felt.

Tim also reports that even after making this sacrifice to stay with his mother, she got worse, not better. So the message is that even if you make a huge sacrifice for someone, it won't work.

It's particularly harmful when a parent openly blames a child for his or her suffering. In Tim's case, his mother repeatedly linked her unhappiness to her children not loving her enough. The guilt he felt must have been intense.

Unfortunately, neither his mother nor his father supported him in his efforts to be strong, capable, and independent. They were simply too absorbed with their own lives and problems to have much left over for their children.

Tim was surprised at how foggy his memory was, although he also knew that he has actively tried to forget a lot of his childhood. His memory had a kind of jerky quality to it, as though we were watching an old black-and-white movie with separate frames and a lot of static. He pointed out that he may just not want to remember life in his house, because although he can recall other things well, he can barely even remember what his parents look like. But the feeling remains: the empty, depressed, pointless sense of loneliness and drifting.

His mother's violent suicide certainly came as a shock to him, and it came as a shock to me in the interview. The dramatic shift in his mood recounting it 20 years later is an indication of how unresolved he is about his relationship with her. Love, anger, guilt, and despair seem all woven together in a way that binds him to his own sense of ambivalence and confusion.

Tim is still seeking and is aware of some repeated patterns. He has tried many ways of helping himself, finding programs and people who are interested in him and his journey, and who offer support and encouragement.

WHAT CAN WE LEARN FROM TIM'S STORY?

I think Tim's story illustrates the power of guilt to bind people long into their adult lives, even when they aren't aware of it. We see, again and again, how the burden was put on him and his siblings to make their mother well, to make her happy, to cater to her, and to put aside any wishes they had to be cared for.

The guilt of failing to help a needy parent plays out in a lot of ways. Here, Tim remains stuck in his own life, not able to live out his own dreams, and also feels stuck and ambivalent about continuing to take care of his girlfriend, who is also needy. He loves her, as he loved his mother, but he is ambivalent about her neediness and dependency. When this kind of guilt is present, people often find themselves in the same kind of relationship repeatedly, despite not consciously wanting to be there.

Children in a family situation like Tim's need to be told, firmly and repeatedly, that a parent's problem is not their fault, it is not their responsibility, and they cannot fix it. Tim and his siblings were left in a situation where they were virtually drenched in blame and guilt. Even if someone couldn't intervene on the children's behalf directly in a physical way, there was no one to even point out to Tim that his mother's unhappiness was certainly not his fault. He can hear it now, as an adult, but his childhood beliefs were firmly implanted and have been part of his psyche for a long time.

We've seen several coping strategies that seem to translate well into adult life and a few that don't. Tim certainly has a lot of creativity and imagination, but it doesn't work so well for him when it takes the form of magical thinking—that is, simply hoping and imagining that somehow, magically, things will get better. He's a bright and creative person, and with less guilt holding him back, he might be able to enjoy his own real strengths and competencies.

Well, you certainly have to wonder what her history was around sexual abuse. Were there other incidents with her that stand out?

There was also abuse by a babysitter when I was about 5 and that's also blurry. Then I was abused again by a close family friend when I was 9 or 10. He was kind of like an uncle for me. I don't remember trying to tell anyone about either of those times, but one of the main points for me is that my mother didn't seem to notice any signs in me that something bad had happened.

I constantly got migraine headaches, I was out of school a lot, and then once I got to be a teenager I discovered heavy metal music, which was great. It was extremely intense and cathartic and helped me get out a lot of feeling.

How else do you think you were coping with all this?

I had a violent temper for a long time. I would take doors off the hinges and throw them across the room. Or I would get sick from just internalizing everything. I would just puke for no reason. Last week a friend of mine e-mailed me a "Question of the day: what does the first day of school remind you of?" My answer: Vomiting!

Public school was not good for me. I didn't understand how things worked, especially once I hit middle school. Elementary school went better probably because there was one teacher in one classroom all day long. And I was in class with the same kids all year long. For the most part I did well. There was a lot of pressure around other boys, though, about how to be cool and I wasn't sure about all that.

Did anyone ever say to you that your mother had problems or ask how things were at home? You were certainly showing some signs of distress.

Nobody. It's an ongoing thing for me that the only people who can see how bad this was are people who have done a lot of therapy or who are therapists. My aunt and my father know my mother really had issues. Nobody ever said to me, this must be tough, your mother has problems, this is difficult. That's one reason it was so confusing. People just think she's a nice, eccentric lady.

I think at some point I realized she had some very weird reactions to things. One incident really stands out, when I was about nine. I was in my mother's room and I was upset about something, and I was crying. My grandmother was in the living room watching TV and she went with this big long loud sigh that meant she was tired of hearing me cry.

And I yelled, " Fuck you lady," which is the first time I had ever said anything like that to her at all. She got up and came into my mom's room, and she laid me out across the bed and she was just hitting me and hitting me, and my mother just left the building. I don't mean literally—but she just stood there. She didn't do anything; she didn't try to stop her; she didn't respond to my crying out. She just left. I remember looking at her and thinking, "Do something!," and she was just completely blank. I don't even remember what happened afterwards. But that was extremely weird.

What happened as you got older and went to middle school?

I remember things changing at home after I got to be a little older. When I was 12 or 13 I started talking back to my grandmother. I started not taking her shit anymore. And at one point she said, "Why are you so mean to me?"

And I said, "*What?* You treat me like a fucking piece of shit!" And I didn't back down, and she didn't say anything else. What was she going to do at that point?

What else were you feeling at that point? How were you coping with things?

My mom wasn't sure what to do because I would have these tantrums. Sometime I would just lose it. This started when I was 11 or 12, and my thoughts would be going incredibly fast that the only thing I could do would be to talk, to slow them down. Because I could only talk so fast and it would make my thoughts go a little bit slower. I put my hand through a window once, to just feel something. Reality was so intensely claustrophobic that I would do whatever it would take to just break that feeling.

I guess if I had been bleeding profusely from somewhere, she might have said, "Maybe we should do something about this." She did do something after I put my hand through a window. She took me to the ER and they asked me, "Who did this?"

And I said, "I did."

And they said, "Why?"

And I thought to myself, "Why not? Why *wouldn't* you put your hand through a window?"

That's the age when I started playing music with some bands, but that was mixed because sometimes it just makes everything more intense, if you're not really dealing with anything.

Did anybody seem to realize you were having a hard time, or did anybody reach out to you? Did you talk to anyone about what was going on?

I called my aunt Barbara once when I just couldn't stand it anymore, and I told her, "My mother is so crazy—I need help!" And she said, "I've got my own problems, and by the way, your mother is bipolar. And these are all the things your grandmother is doing that are making me crazy." She started talking about that. I realized she wasn't talking

about the mean grandmother, Nana; she was talking about the good grandmother!

I said, "Wait a minute, wait a minute—you're telling me about
Nonny??" And she said, "Yes."

"You've got the wrong person. Nonny is definitely eccentric and weird,
I agree, but she's been a fucking saving grace for me!"

*Did your mother, with all her problems, ever seem to recognize that you
were having a hard time, that you might need some more help?*

I told my mother about being so speeded up and talking to slow down,
when I was a kid, and she listened to me, but she didn't really have anything to say. Like she didn't say to herself, "Gee, my son is doing this;
maybe he's having a nervous breakdown!" (Laughs)

*What was school like for you, once you got into middle school and then
high school?*

The pressures of trying to fit in in middle school were overwhelming. It
seemed like all the cliques of kids developed overnight and I wasn't part
of any of it. There was a lot of pressure from the boys at school and from
the male teachers to be a certain kind of way. I didn't understand all the
rules; they made no sense to me. It was strange and overwhelming, going
from one class to another according to some schedule I didn't get. The
cookie-cutter system did not work for me at all. There was no freedom
and I wasn't learning anything.

*Did you have any male role models, anyone you could talk to or who you
looked up to?*

It's been a huge thing for me that I didn't have a male role model. I went
to an alternative high school at 16 or 17, and that's the first time I had any
male role models that were good and caring. They put me in my place
when I needed to be put in my place, but they also loved me and were
good to me.

But other places where I might have found role models didn't work for
me. I quit the Catholic Church when I was 14, and also the Boy Scouts.
They both seemed oppressive and there were so many rules, and I also
didn't like competing with other kids.

I was getting interested in music at that point, and I was a creative
kid. I was starting to get interested in meditation and Eastern philosophy.
I tried to talk to the priest about it, but he looked at me like I was talking
about Satan or something.

*Were you still in contact with your father at this point? How was your
relationship with him?*

My father wanted me to come and live with him when I was in high school, but I didn't want to leave the friends I had made. Also, although the system I had was broken, it was the system I was used to. I didn't want to have to go to another school and make new friends.

I'm really glad I made that decision, because if I had gone to live with them I would've gone to a school that was very good and incredibly competitive. So he saw what was going on, but he didn't really know what to do about it. He knew my mother was crazy.

What were things like at home with your grandmother during this time?

My grandmother died when I was 14, from a heart attack. Before she died, she apologized to my mother and said to her, "Tell Josh I'm sorry; I didn't know any better; I didn't know what I was doing." But I was infuriated because she never in my whole life had apologized to me for anything. I thought, "How dramatic to apologize on your deathbed!" and she never even said it to me. I was really glad that she died. I thought to myself, "Finally."

The only apology I ever got was a lemon square and a brownie. And even now I have a terribly hard time saying that I'm sorry. Like if I do something I have to do and it hurts the other person, I can't say that I'm sorry for doing it. I'm working on it.

Things were a little lighter in the house after she died, but the damage was already done. My mother had already been into the New Agey things, but she just went further with it after her mother died. Actually, I did too for a while. I told her to go to therapy, but she would just say, "I don't have anything to talk about."

What were some things you were doing to cope with your feelings? They were pretty raw a lot of the time, it sounds like.

I wrote, which I still do, but I wrote a lot of violent stories and stuff, and sometimes I wrote out skits and had them performed. As a teenager, I started writing skits and seeing them done on stage and it was really helpful. But at some point I realized it could be endless. Now I write more about the absurdity of all of it.

And what was happening with you as you were getting to the age of leaving home?

I started to remember the sexual abuse just before it was time to leave. I started having flashbacks when I was 18 or 19, and I was angry all the time. That was weird for me. I was just furious all the time and I couldn't figure it out. Then after a while I started having actual memories of the abuse. And I told my mother and she didn't know what to do. I didn't want her to confront this family friend who was one of the guys who had abused me, because I was afraid of what he would do to her. I had a lot of symptoms once I left home.

What were those like?

I started to have racing thoughts again, and I'd have to talk in real time to slow myself down. I'd have to say to myself, "Slow down, this is how fast the world is really going." And then I could actually slow down. Like when I was younger, except I was aware this meant that something was not okay with me.

How did things go when it was time for you to go to college?

In a way, when I went to college I wanted to get as far away from home as I could. But at the same time, I really missed being home. Once I was there though, I started doing these weekend warrior workshop kinds of things. There was heavy confrontation and of course none of the leaders were trained, but I thought it was awesome! I mean there was truth in there and it was kind of like a therapy form of punk rock. I did this for years.

I also got into a men's group, which was really helpful. I could also see how they pushed things way too fast to really resolve them. But I started to realize that the relationship with my mother was pretty incestuous.

How did you think of it, once you were away and more on your own?

I became disillusioned about it. The illusion I had was that my mother and I had a really good close relationship, and that she was really a good and solid person who really cared about me and got me. So I started to see the other parts of the relationship more clearly, even though I was still baffled about it. So even though she was sweet a lot of times, that was outweighed by the times that she just wasn't protective. It was kind of like putting together a jigsaw puzzle.

Were you in contact with her during those college years?

Yeah, even though my relationship with her was changing and she was changing. She got heavily into numerology. She was fascinated with numbers and with little categories and boxes that she could fit people into. She got totally obsessed with that.

What were you doing at that point to deal with the memories you were having of the abuse?

I didn't want to go the "victim" route. I have a lot of feelings about that whole culture. But one thing was to try to warn the daughter of the family friend who had abused me, because by now she had two little girls. I had my mother listen in on the phone call while I told this woman that her father had abused me as a child and that she should be aware of that because she had young children. She just said, "Oh, I'll take this to my grave!"—which was the worst thing she could have said. I told her to go talk to somebody.

What's your relationship been like with your mother since then?

I realized in my early 20s that I had to stop being in contact with her. She just made me crazy. When I talked to her on the phone I just felt like I was in another reality. There've been a number of times I've tried to explain to her why I don't want to talk to her. I told her, "If you want to understand what I'm going through, what our dynamic is, then read this book, *Emotional Incest*, and I gave her the book. So she got in touch with me after a while and said, "I read the book, but I don't see what's wrong with it."

I've had so many conversations with her, where she asks, "Look, just explain to me why you don't want to talk to me." And I've explained it to her three or four times: "You treated me like your friend, your husband, your therapist, everything. Not like your child. That's not normal. You didn't see what was happening to me right in front of your eyes. I can't go on being in communication with you unless you realize there was something off about that. All I'm asking is for some acknowledgment that maybe it was difficult for me. I'm not even asking for an apology." And she has no idea what I'm talking about. She's just not capable.

I have contacted her on and off since I was 21, so there have been some times when I've talked to her over the years. The agreement is, if something's really, really wrong, if someone's dead, if someone's dying—then call me. Otherwise, no. I helped her out when she had heart surgery. I went and handled the bills and took care of stuff for her.

Have there been times you've tried again to have contact?

When I came back from Seattle a few years ago, I decided to give it another shot. So I let her meet Kris, my wife, and Kris was kind of grossed out by it. She said my mother was looking at me with this longing look, like her life depended on me. It turned out that my mother cornered Kris and started asking her all these questions like, "When did you get married? When you were born? What was the exact date? Don't tell Josh I asked you this! Don't tell Josh I asked you these questions."

So I told my dad, and my dad was really disappointed because he said he thought maybe she had changed. And I told him, "She's not going to change; she is the way she is. Now can you leave me alone about this? I can't have contact with her anymore—it makes me crazy and I'm dealing with it. So just leave it alone." And he has for the most part.

When other people ask you about her, how do you explain why you're not in contact?

I have to really stand my ground with people who question me. People feel free to say, "It's your mother; you have to make up with her." I have a couple of friends who really get it, but most people don't. It can be very wearing to have to defend myself on this. I usually just end up saying, "Well, you deal with your mother and I'll deal with mine."

My mother would want to consume me if she could. She'd take anything I had to give and just want more and more. She tracks me through my website and everything else, so she'll send me little notes—"I know you were just in Colorado, congratulations on that good review"—and I just want to throw up.

I'm a professional writer and I use social media. I post on Facebook; I blog; I share my experiences online. It's what I do as a professional and I'm not going to stop because she's reading it.

How are things with your father now?

I like to see him, but I told him, "Look, here's the deal. I cannot change who you are—I get that. But when I visit you, you can't drink. Not even a sip. Because when you drink you become a person I don't like." He and my stepmother start drinking in the afternoon, and by evening they're plastered and there are young kids running around that they're supposed to be watching. I can't control that, but I can control when I visit and when I don't.

And he'll drive when he's drunk, and the last thing I need is, first, for my father to die. And second, to kill someone else and then die on top of it! He says it won't happen, but I know it could. But I love my dad and want to hold onto that connection—but there have to be those boundaries in place.

What's it been like for you, to not have your father as a male role model? How have you thought about that and coped with that?

It's hard for me to reach out to other men when I'm really depressed. That's a pretty scary state, and I like to be able to talk to other guys, but I have to be careful how I approach it. It's really hard to find friends who aren't at one extreme or the other, either too New Agey or too macho. There's just a lot of miscommunication that happens with men when we're trying to talk about things. A lot of times it's easier with women.

What are some of the things that have been the most helpful for you, going through all this and also trying to work with it creatively, in your writing?

One really important thing has been finding the right therapist. A therapist who really gets who I am and understands what I'm trying to do. I've had a lot of therapists, and the one I'm working with now is the one who's been the most helpful. And that's the one that my wife and I talk to. You also do really need a community, friends, people you really trust and you can talk to. You can't do this stuff by yourself.

And the thing that my wife and I are working on in couples therapy is to individuate more from each other, and I'm also trying to be clearer about understanding myself.

I know for me there's a lot of guilt around the fact that I can't always get it all together. And I have to realize that sometimes things are just shitty; I just have to get through it. There's no golden ticket; there's no shortcut. I've been thinking for years, "Well, once I get through this, then I'll be okay" and then later, "Well, once I get through *this*, then I'll be okay," and it just doesn't happen that way.

Another thing that helps a lot is being on an antidepressant. I can go into these episodes every once in a while where I'm just flat out. I can't do anything. Then I ruminate and get down on myself and eventually I start to feel suicidal. And that scares me! So I finally did some serious reading on depression and I realized—there's mental illness on my mother's side of the family, and I'm at risk and I'm done with pretending it's not serious.

So I'm done with 5HTP; I'm done with shamanic voyages as a way to get through depression. (Laughs) Not that those things aren't helpful, but I've got to figure out my limitations and what's healthy for me. I have to take care of myself.

I grew up in a volatile, hyperemotional environment. Now I really like to live out here in the woods. My nervous system gets shot really fast. I have very low tolerance for a lot of simulation. So I work in the city, but I have to live out here. I get overwhelmed really quickly. I've been hypervigilant my entire life. It's really hard for me to feel safe. So I have to figure out what I want and need in my life, and I have to pay attention to that.

Is there anything else you want to say about the process of getting through this, how it's been for you and how it still is for you?

There is a way to get better, but it is a very winding road. And it's okay to be really confused, really baffled, and seriously angry. There's this scene in *Barfly*, the movie on Charles Bukowski when he's walking by this car and there's this dog in the car, just going at him, just wanting to kill him, and just barking and raging and throwing himself against the window. And Bukowski says, "Wow. That's a piece of art." You have to accept that you can feel that kind of anger.

A lot of times I've really given up. I've given up on myself and I've given up on the world. I've given up on other people. And I think there's something really good about that because it lets you get to the other side of it.

There are moments when I feel some kind of safety or connection with other people and I love those moments, but they're so intangible and so unique to each person. I really didn't experience it growing up, or maybe a few moments here and there.

ABOUT JOSH: MY REFLECTIONS

Here's a description of a mother who is both intrusive and also neglectful. My guess is that she was a good-enough mother to the very young infant and toddler Josh and that gave him some of his ability to survive emotionally and to make his way through a very confusing growing-up. Some of his bafflement, I think, is because his mother is not at all aggressive or malevolent, or even undermining. She is simply not up the task of protecting a child who is in danger, nor of seeing dangerous situations for him or for herself.

I shared with Josh my impression that his mother sounded dissociated sometimes, especially the time when he was beaten by his grandmother, her mother. The fact that she often forgot things after these "blank" periods pretty much confirms that she was dissociating. This is not an uncaring mother; this may be a mother who has been traumatized and whose automatic defense has been simply to "go away" in her mind to avoid overwhelming pain and fear.

Her lack of boundaries with Josh and her own defenses against trauma lead her to want to absorb him into her own self so that they are merged and he is her companion. This is why she is so confusing. She does in fact "mean well," but she's operating entirely inside a psychological system that cannot protect her or him, and in which there's a lot of distortion about who is who and what is what.

She has a reason to have created this distortion, but Josh doesn't distort his own perceptions in that way, so when his grandmother hits him he protests and knows that his parent should be protecting him. When it doesn't happen, he is baffled. He knows it should be otherwise.

His "going crazy" when talking to his mother also suggests that the only way to relate to her is inside her own skewed world, where nothing bad ever happens to anyone and there are no threats or dangers anywhere. Because Josh knows that reality is otherwise, it's very difficult to relate to her. Therefore he chooses to cut off contact. She simply cannot see him as separate—not because she is malevolent or willfully destructive, but because seeing him as separate threatens her own sense of psychological integrity.

This is truly a confusing parent. Although she doesn't wish harm, she causes great harm. Although she wants only the best for Josh, she doesn't see who he is. She wants to connect with him, but only on her own terms. She is loving, she is intrusive, and she is neglectful. He feels, in some way, loved, but also intruded upon and deeply neglected and unprotected.

WHAT CAN WE LEARN FROM JOSH'S STORY?

Josh has a lot to teach about boundaries, how hard they can be to put in place and how important they are. Family cut-offs shouldn't be done lightly, but sometimes a cut-off is not only essential to the person who initiates it but also a good way to reset the boundaries in a difficult relationship. A cut-off can be the *only* way a person feels any power to control a relationship, and it can also signal to the offending party that the situation is serious and the consequences for violation are real. With people who routinely and thoughtlessly violate boundaries, this can be a brand-new concept: that a boundary is a "no" that will be enforced.

Sometimes the person who initiates the cut-off tries again and allows for contact with the person he or she has disconnected from. What happens then is very important and signals whether there's been any real and lasting change. Josh tried that, and his mother did exactly what she had done before, as though he had never talked to her. So his cut-off was not impulsive and happened only after he'd tried many times to explain himself and had given her a chance to act in a more respectful way that's reasonable. I think it's also important that the cut-off is not intended as a punishment of her but a protection for him.

His experience of being challenged about this cut-off is very common. There's a general expectation that difficulties between parents and children can be resolved and that people should just keep trying. People like Josh often need some confirmation that their decision is valid and reasonable.

Josh also teaches us that, for some people, creative expression is a huge factor in repairing old damage. Josh's work centers around seeing things clearly and also turning them this way and that, to capture all the ways in which the "usual" world can be seen. He has created a body of work based on his intelligence, humor, and ability to deal with a lot of contradictory "realities." He's had plenty of practice, and he's putting it to good use.

11

Randall: "My first memory? Her trying to strangle me"

Randall lives in the Northeast, is married, and is in his early 60s. He has worked as a city planner for many years. Randall was very generous in sharing his long and complex story. His unusual childhood was punctuated with several incidents of sexual abuse, including sexual abuse by his mother. She was highly accomplished but quite disturbed and narcissistic. Randall fragmented into a number of different "parts" as a child and was diagnosed as an adult with DID, formerly called multiple personality disorder. His journey to healing and integration is remarkable, especially since he also has a successful career and a long and happy marriage.

Can you write a bit about yourself and your family, to give us a starting point?

I'm the younger of two kids with a brother six years older. Because of my parents' work, I grew up for several years on the Hopi/Navaho Reservation in Arizona where my father worked as a supervisor of social workers. My mother was a physician and was a hospital administrator while we lived there.

We lived on the government compound on the reservation, but I was fortunate to have American Indian caretakers throughout these years. The Hopi culture fosters tremendous love for children, and I still remember the warmth, the love, and the concern that these women had for me.

They were with me for 10 or 11 hours a day and I think they gave me what they would call the "seed corn" that enabled me to survive emotionally.

We moved several times after we left Arizona and ended up in South Dakota where we lived from the time I was 6 until I left home at 17. I knew very early that my mother worked and that she "did not need to," and we certainly did not fit the model of the American family at the time because she wasn't a teacher, a nurse, or a secretary.

What do you know about your extended family?

My father was from an affluent farming family in the Midwest, and he was the "rocket scientist" success story of his generation. Because of my advanced degrees, I'm the rocket scientist of my own generation. He had a much older brother, who seemed to be a gentle nice guy until he sexually abused me. He also had a younger sister who was a suspiciously well-off "executive secretary" who eventually married after a long string of affairs with her bosses. My parents met when my father got a job with my mother's father, who was a very well-known and well-respected researcher in child advocacy.

My mother grew up with a fair degree of financial privilege because of her father's work, but I know little about her emotional life growing up or about what would have made her become such a destructive person. She had a younger brother whom I liked, and he was generous and easygoing. When we visited either set of grandparents, it seemed obligatory and I don't recall any sense of affection or warmth.

What happened the first time you knew something was wrong with your mother?

I was probably three when I must have been making too much noise in a playpen, and my mother grabbed me by the neck and started strangling me. I remember her grabbing me with both her hands around my neck, her rageful face in mine as she held me up by my neck and shook me. Then I remember being in a daze on the floor after I came back to consciousness. I was alone on the floor and heard my mother furiously banging around pots and pans in the kitchen.

There was a second moment as well. I was about five, and I had a male "babysitter," a farm boy from rural Minnesota who was a grad student. His "care" ultimately extended to sexual abuse, which started with "touch" and then moved on to more graphic abuse. After much trepidation I went to my mother, and in the language of a five-year-old tried to tell her that something "weird" was going on. My mother listened to me, then flew into a rage. She shrieked that I must be making these stories up and that it was all my fault—a conflict of logic that I actually understood at that age. She ended the discussion by slapping me in the face and walking away, leaving me stunned, sitting on the floor, and knowing that I was doomed. So his sexual abuse continued and even intensified all that year until we moved, eventually including my older brother in several incidents of what amounted to gang rapes.

Did you ever tell anyone about the earlier physical abuse by your mother?

Absolutely not. There was no one to tell, save the Hopi housekeepers. I am certain that by the age of three, I felt I was "in this alone."

These are devastating events for a child. How else did you see your mother acting or talking that seemed "off"?

She never really seemed to look at me, or at the person she was speaking to, and she talked incessantly about academic success and how superior our family was and so on. She had something to say about everything and everyone. You didn't have a conversation with her; she just preached. Also, her moods were profoundly unpredictable and changed with lightning speed.

How did others in the family relate to her? How did your father relate to her?

I think my father was terrified of her. He seemed to be shut down at home. I remember him reading the paper and later, watching the news, with the ever-present amber glass of iced beverage [bourbon]. He did not participate in dinner "conversations," which my mother led around current events at school or in the community. When he did, it was to rip out a caustic or sarcastic comment that was surgically accurate and insightful; then he would observe the impact of his comment, then retreat to silence.

My brother seemed both drawn to her and terrified of her. She lavished a great deal of attention on him.

You mentioned a connection with your mother's younger brother—was there any contact with him during these younger years?

When I was 11 or so, my brother and I spent a summer at his home, taking swimming lessons and generally having a good time. He was a warm, congenial guy and I think he wanted to give my brother and me some different experiences. At his house, there was laughter, there was playfulness, and Uncle James talked *with* me, not *at* me. Children were allowed to laugh and be quite boisterous.

What was a typical daily routine when you were a child?

I would make myself breakfast, then my parents would show up in the kitchen and have the same argument they always did about his cooking eggs for her that she didn't want. I would duck out and leave for school.

I walked to school, and I played the piano and cello, so music classes and the community orchestra were distractions that kept me after school and away from home. Later, in high school, I was part of the debate team, and that too required lots of practices and the wonderful grace of some weekends out of town.

When did you realize that your family was different from other kids' families?

I didn't have all that much to compare it to until later on, when I realized that other families talked to each other and seemed to be concerned about each other, or to enjoy each other's company. For a long time it seemed we were different by being superior, mostly because my mother was a doctor. And don't forget I was hearing constantly that we were better than the other people in this community, that they were not our "intellectual peers." However, I thought these people did not seem that dumb to me, just rural.

But my role as a kid meant never to invite anyone home, keep out of trouble, don't do anything that would embarrass my parents—like sports or hanging around with other kids.

My mother also had rigid dietary rules all week, and Sunday evenings were the only times we could have food that anybody else would think of as snacks—like popcorn, coke, ice cream. I loved that freedom once a week.

How did you cope with all this?

I spent a tremendous amount of time reading, when I was not doing homework, and I played in my room with blocks. I built houses, buildings, and small towns with a focus on space and layout and knew the words "city planning" and "architecture" by the time I was about eight. Generally, I played by myself.

Sports were seen as rowdy, dirty, and messy. Blue jeans were to be worn for household chores, not for recreation. So joining or participating in school athletics was out of the question.

Were there neighbors or other families around who might have given you some break from your family life at home?

My parents didn't socialize much, because of our supposed superiority to people in town. So we didn't really have connections in the neighborhood or in town.

My mother had no real friends as I understand friendship now. There was one neighbor who had coffee with my mother once a week, and sometimes I overheard them talking. Later on my mother complained about the inanity of the conversation and the intellectual limitations of the community that we lived in. I felt sorry for the neighbor lady, who was just looking for some companionship and coffee, not a dialogue about Proust.

You've mentioned your father's quietness and also his drinking—was that anything that was ever talked about or a source of argument?

When I got a little older it became blindingly obvious that both of them were alcoholics. They hid it from each other, let alone anyone else. My father had his bourbon and my mother had her wine "to help her sleep." But long before I had that concept, I did feel that something was "different." One did not ask Dad a serious question after his first amber glass, and one did not ask Mother questions after dinner. They were busy reading and, quietly, drinking and drinking and drinking. My mother hid hers more successfully: Gallo wine jugs in her bedroom closet. I discovered those at the age of about eight or so (What were cases of wine doing in the bedroom closet rather than in the basement where we stored extra food? An open question and one I dared not ask). My father was rarely without a drink in his hand.

That helped me see in retrospect why they seemed to prefer isolation. They didn't join the local country club because the social part of it was "inane" and the golf or swimming were "a waste of time" and to be looked down on. I think both of them were terrified of any kind of casual unplanned social contact.

You've painted a good picture of how your parents were. How were you feeling during this period. How were you coping with living this way?

A significant portion of my childhood was spent on not antagonizing my mother and in not being a point of negative attention or focus in any way at home, at school, or on the playground. I took on a persona of "background," "low key," "speak when spoken to," focusing entirely on risk-averse behaviors.

And it would have been unthinkable to talk to anyone outside or inside the family. Anywhere I lived, my parents were respected professionals in the community, and my mother's demeanor as "Dr. Ann," was formidable and intimidating.

How did you cope with times you were upset?

I dissociated. I fragmented and split. I had a few different "personalities" that showed up then. The official term for it is "DID"—dissociative identity disorder, which is or was my diagnosis. It used to be called multiple personality disorder. It usually comes out of a background of multiple kinds of abuse including sexual abuse. So when I look back, I see one personality—the placid, self-effacing, soft-spoken "little Ricky." This part "fronted" and was, for all intents and purposes, the kid that my parents knew. My understanding now is that "Ricky" appeared after my mother tried to strangle me, when I realized that I wasn't safe if I didn't watch my step every minute. Playing or making noise could get me killed.

There was also another part, "Jake," who went "underground" and planned our escape from my family. By the age of 10 or 11, that part of me was aggressively planning the most effective and least controversial way out—going to college, far, far away from home. Even at that early age I was looking at college catalogs and planning where to go. Because I was isolated from my peers, I didn't realize how unusual that was.

Another part, identified much later as "Rudderow," had a surprising ability for caustic sarcasm. My mother avoided me when I seemed to be in that frame of mind, and my brother would end up crying if I got him out of earshot of either parent. He stopped sexually abusing me at just about that time, and I think my ability to retaliate that way was the reason he stopped.

I know that I had parts that were profoundly upset. Those parts I hid. If I showed pain, fear, or anger, it would have been giving ammunition to the enemy.

What were you aware of at that time, before you had the language for knowing you really had several different personas?

My life seemed to be about escaping, getting out, moving away, and about seeming to be a quiet inoffensive boy until I could do that.

There were some horrific things that happened that I only remembered years later. I think at the time I just "forgot" them as soon as I could because there was no place to put them. One was when I was 7 and my brother was 13, he and our cousin played "cops and robbers" with me during one of the visits to Ohio. As a result, I was handcuffed as a prisoner and then raped. When I fought back, they essentially attacked me. (Years later a doctor asked me how long ago I had broken several ribs, and I flashed back to that scene. Until that moment I had no idea I had ever broken any ribs or that such a thing could be determined decades after the fact.)

Later, during the same visit, my uncle came into the bedroom that I was using (it had been, eerily, my father's bedroom in his youth) and sodomized me. My mother sensed something, and we spent a long afternoon in the parlor of the farmhouse while she waited for me to talk. But I no longer trusted her at all, and I stonewalled her, despite my physical and emotional pain.

This was your father's older brother?

Yes, the one I had uneasy feelings about anyway. Later I thought that what happened to me had probably also happened to my father when he was a kid. His brother was a lot older than him, just like my brother.

So even at that young age you had shut down to your mother, even when she seemed to be showing concern.

Definitely, because she was just not trustworthy. It was only two years before that that she had screamed at me when I said the babysitter was doing something wrong with me.

That's such a huge event for a child to have to deal with alone. Is it your understanding now that you had different split-off personalities that kept the trauma out of consciousness?

I started having flashbacks and memories in college, and had very intense reactions when somebody in a conversation mentioned "male rape." But that's later on—at this time I would say I just removed it from my conscious mind as soon as I could, knowing subconsciously that I couldn't "remember" it and function, and there was no way to deal with it then.

What else do you recall about what was going on for you in the family?

I know I was terrified of my mother and her moods and her potential for rage. In public, she was well known as "Dr. Ann," and she carried her education and her big vocabulary like a club.

There was one exception to her austere, judgmental approach towards me. She administered enemas to me from as early as I can remember to about the age of eight. Her mood was different: her voice shifted to some kind of warmth, and she seemed to care. She abruptly decided to stop doing it when I was about eight and of course never talked about it at all.

Was there ever any indication that she had a problem of any kind, that there was anything objectively wrong with her behavior or her moods, anything like that? Did anyone ever say "she's stressed" or "she's high-strung"?

No. My family was like an island. There were some schoolteachers who, I felt, sensed that something was off. I had a few teachers along the way who seemed to like me and gave me interesting challenges. But nothing was ever said.

Did you have friends? Would you have them come to your house? If so, what did they think of your mother?

In grade school I did become friends with a neighbor, whose home I visited. His father traveled a lot and his mother "held down the fort" and prepared meals and gossip with equal zeal. There was laughter in their home. But she never made reference to my mother.

Some kids having a hard time at home kind of "adopt" another family, or another family adopts them and they spend a lot of time together. Was that the case with this neighbor family?

No, that wouldn't have been acceptable to my mother. I think the occasional visit didn't provoke her anger, but anything more would have.

What was school like for you?

School was an escape and a relief, a way to not be at home. My older brother, who was exceptionally bright, was also rebellious and verbally antagonistic. So they seemed to assume I would be the same way. When I focused on getting good grades and not causing any trouble, they realized how different we were. When I took up music and debate, school was even a better place for me.

Are there other things that stand out in early adolescence?

When I hit puberty, my mother began to enter my bedroom when I was asleep, or she thought I was asleep, and would begin to caress my lower torso and/or my legs, approaching my privates in the process. I was, of course, vigilantly wide awake, once I knew these were standard occurrences, and learned to feign sleep.

How did you react to this bizarre intrusion?

Internally, I "went out of body," levitating to a corner of the bedroom to maintain a bird's-eye view of the activities, seeing—and smelling—my mother with her drunken breath, approaching my bed and feeling me up. She did, at times, touch my privates, and I learned how to dissociate sufficiently as to avoid arousal on any level (including the physical), as a way of discouraging her. This nighttime sexual abuse wasn't violent like the abuse by my brother or cousin or babysitter, but in retrospect, it seems to me to have been the creepiest.

She also insisted on our "going out for dinner" when my father was out of town on business. She would insist on my being her escort and going to the most lavish place in town. We would make an "entrance" and have dinner together. It was creepy, and I think of it now as some kind of emotional incest.

Later on I also realized or remembered—another blinding flash of the obvious—that my parents had removed the doors to both my brother's and my bedrooms and replaced them with cheap folding vinyl accordion doors, which couldn't be really closed or locked at all but left us both with zero privacy.

That would suggest that both you and your brother were potentially in a very vulnerable situation. Did you have any sense of that or was this something you only put together later?

I put it together later. At the time I didn't have much to do with my brother, or as little as I could have. We were quite opposite—he was rebellious and I stayed out of trouble and channeled my energy into "getting the fuck outta Dodge" by sending "Ricky" to school for good grades. My brother ended up being mired in South Dakota, having antagonized every authority figure he encountered.

What was your relationship like with your mother during your teen years?

"Ricky," the dissociated part that was more or less present for daily life, was quiet and self-effacing. But one incident stands out a lot. My parents decided I should go to camp, and instead of something outdoors I managed to convince them I could go to debate camp for six weeks. That was actually a good reflection on them and a trial run for me at being free.

So at 16 I took the train to Chicago by myself and when I arrived I realized a lot of the kids going to the camp were being dropped off by their parents. I was puzzled—parents did that kind of thing??

I imagine there may have been a lot more surprises along the way.

Another debate camper got a call from her parents because her brother, a helicopter pilot, had just been reported as MIA in Vietnam. She cried and had many long phone calls with her parents. I was startled at the nature of the emotion and that she could share it with her parents. I think I was envious. It was very different—this care, this concern, this awareness, and this articulation of feelings.

That moment was thrown in stark contrast when, two weeks into the six-week curriculum, my father had a heart attack, at age 53, and it took a very long time to get to a hospital. He was in bad shape. My mother called me, not that day or the day after, but *three days later*, to inform me that it had been "a close call." Stunned, I did not know how to act, but the contrast between my family and the young woman I just described could not have been sharper.

We agreed, in our brief phone call, that I should stay at the debate camp—no reason to "cave" to the sentiment that I might want to see my dad, confirm with my own eyes that he was still alive. When camp was over and I saw my dad, we just shook hands as always.

I got very concerned about my father's health and about what would happen if he died. I knew he had some level of concern for me. I did something I'd never done before—when I got home from debate camp I secretly went through his financial papers and learned that if he died, my mother would have total control over all the finances. I knew then that whatever college I chose, I would have to make sure I could swing it on my own if she pulled out financial support. So I ended up going to the only school where I could get enough scholarship money if I needed to.

Given your mother's apparent possessiveness, if we can call it that, what happened when you got to the age of dating?

My mother disapproved of my dating, and since I was a tall, skinny geek, it didn't happen much. I did date one girl, and my mother disparaged her motives and my father flirted incessantly. The girl, who was intelligent and sociable, thought my parents were bizarre and we decided not to spend time at my house anymore.

Were there other adults who helped you out or provided some other presence in your life?

I had a few teachers who were encouraging and supportive, and who didn't seem all that intimidated by my mother. My debate coach was the best, seeming to recognize that I didn't have much in the way of family. He viewed his debate team as a kind of surrogate family for all of us, and those are the only pictures of me at that age that show me smiling.

How did your parents react to your success in debating? Did they come to see any debates or support you in any way?

I hid my success from my mother to avoid criticism. I also lied about what events parents could attend, to make sure they didn't try to do so. She would have had to find something to diminish about it. So, support? Not at all.

I think most of the people who knew my mother were terrified of her, her manner, her sense of presence, her education, and her incredibly sharp tongue. I suspect that some felt sorry for me but also stayed away from me, fearful of somehow incurring this woman's wrath.

Did you have friends that you confided in or felt close to?

I knew a few kids who I liked and who liked me, but there wasn't anyone close or any "best friend" to confide in. And certainly no group of friends to hang around with—that would have been "a waste of time."

Were you aware that you had split-off parts of yourself that reacted differently and felt differently?

I was aware that the part of me who went to school was, according to other parts, a bit of a "goody two-shoes," but that was necessary to be able to get away eventually. I was aware that there were some dark memories somewhere.

Decades later when I was diagnosed with DID, I found I was in the middle of the dissociative spectrum. I didn't "lose time" and I was aware of the different aspects of my personality, but I couldn't control switching from one to the other. I knew it was happening—that was all.

How did things go when you went off to college after all your planning? Were you comfortable with it?

Yes!!! It was a lifeline, a dream, and an essential act of self-preservation. I knew that I was jumping off the diving board, but figured that I would learn how to slice the water when I "hit." There was no real alternative except to stay enmeshed in the family dysfunction and turn into a drunk, which I was aware that my brother was doing.

Once you got some distance, how did you see your family?

I realized they were alcoholics, and also that they had chosen South Dakota and then spent all their time saying how inferior it was. I started to see how they just protected themselves from other people and created an artificial world of superiority, living their lives in an "intellectual wilderness," as they saw it.

Were there any changes at home, when you went back for vacations and so forth?

My father started to drink less as my mother had more problems, as though he had to retreat into alcohol when she was at full throttle. After she died it was confirmed that she had started to develop very early Alzheimer's around that time. I don't know why they stayed together because there was never any visible affection.

Back to you at college—how was it for you once you got settled in?

In the first few days at college, I looked at the bleak dorm room, furnished with beat-up junky dorm furniture and stacks of books, and said to myself that "this is my home." Now that I was 17, my home was wherever I was. My home was with me, for better or worse, *not* with my parents. This translated to my telling them that I would be visiting them in their home, a phrase that did not go unnoticed and drove my mother nuts. "This is your home too," she would say, followed by dead silence on my part. That thought, that my home was where I was, not where my parents were, was incredibly powerful.

On some level, I knew I was safe. No one was going to gang-rape me here; no one was going to go into a drunken groping binge in my bedroom; and the harshest critics on the faculty could in no way approach my mother's disdain, and in fact my teachers were mostly complimentary. It seemed very odd.

I could exhale. For the first time in my life, I did not need to be vigilant 24/7. It was hard to let go, sometimes almost a giddy feeling of relief that I could not understand. I had a chance to let my mind run free of criticism, and that was an amazing, amazing experience. My grades ranged from A to D for the first time because I was letting myself focus on the things I liked and letting the other things fall by the wayside.

How did things go for you socially at college?

I began to make some friends and had a couple of girlfriends. I wasn't completely all there, of course, because of the dissociation. But I was much more free than when I lived with my parents.

Did you understand at that time that you had multiple parts and that only some of them had any real voice?

I think the only way that came out was in my artwork. I discovered real art, a classroom with canvas and the ability to let my subconscious be expressed. I did a huge painting of a woman, nude, that was very predatory—what a surprise! Not that it was conscious. Then I did a self-portrait. It looked like a gaunt, mature man with one side of his face and upper torso cast in light, the other in pitch black. I had no idea at the time that unconsciously I was painting myself as a dissociated being— the white parts were public; the black parts were almost invisible but still present.

So I guess the answer is, I did know but not consciously. It came through in all these other ways though.

What was happening emotionally for you during college? It's pretty hard to keep that psychological stuff completely under wraps.

My feeling of freedom and independence was a breath of fresh air, then a breeze and then a wind. But you're right, things started to come up that I didn't know how to deal with. In a freshman bullshit session, I got triggered or activated and didn't realize it.

I got up to take a walk, and as I walked I went into a period of about six hours of complete amnesia, forgetting who I was, where I was. After several hours of walking, I eventually realized that I was on a college campus and that I thus must be a student and maybe I would find a building that would be familiar. I happened on my main classroom building, and when I saw my name on a drafting board, my memory suddenly returned in a massive internal whirlwind.

It had been six or eight hours that I had completely lost. It was terrifying. The thing that had set me off was a comment about male rape— I finally remembered this years later in an EMDR session in the trauma therapy I finally sought out. [EMDR is a specialized trauma therapy in which old memories can sometimes emerge in the way Randall describes here.]

Did these memories manifest in other ways? And did they interfere with how you were doing in school? I know they can be very debilitating.

I avoided sleeping on a bed, preferring the floor. I managed to keep my bed messed up with books and clothes, realizing years later that, for parts of me, beds were associated with rape, and if I did not sleep in one, I could avoid molestation. I passed it off as "bohemian."

I was a junior when I had my first "body memories." Moments after waking I would be temporarily paralyzed from the knees down. Later it was obvious that it was a body memory of my mother's sexual abuse. Nobody knew what it was at that time though, so I went to a neurologist and had a lot of tests before someone at college recommended therapy. I was in group therapy, and even though the abuse memories didn't surface, it was good to be able to talk about some emotional things and to realize therapy could help.

I began to see how different my family was emotionally. Other kids had families with emotions, tears, laughter, jokes, teasing, and I had parents who dropped me off with a brisk handshake. I started to see that some people have these strange things called "emotions" and that it was safe to know that and to realize that, and there was no one to chastise me. Other kids had lengthy conversations by phone with distant family members, while I carefully called on Saturday morning when both parents would still be sober.

What happened as you came closer to graduating and leaving college? Did you have a plan, or did your parents have some plan for you?

My parents came to my graduation, but because I only received several honors and awards, and did not make Phi Beta Kappa, my mother was contemptuous. When I got my second degree a few years later, with academic accomplishments most parents would be proud of, I didn't invite them. It seemed pointless and I didn't want them there.

* * *

How did you fare emotionally and functionally after you began your own life postcollege?

I had done well in school and interned with a prestigious city planning firm. So immediately I had a good job, work friends, and an independent life. From there I moved several times, and also spent some time in the military, but had some significant depression and heavy drinking.

How did you manage your family interactions during that time?

I continued to live as far away as possible and called my parents once a month. Once they came to New York City to visit, and I think they were surprised and my father even impressed that I handled myself with confidence and ease. He commented that I had evidently made some very good choices in education, jobs, and so forth. It was a rare moment of validation.

How were you doing emotionally?

"Ricky" was still the hardworking guy who did his job. So my dissociation worked well in that way. But I developed an overwhelming compulsion to visit gay bathhouses and have sex with other men. It was about my being in charge and of course a kind of reenactment of some of the sexual abuse but at my instigation. Afterwards I would go home and shower for at least an hour, then the next day be back at work for a 12-hour day. I also had other more acceptable activities where I was seen as the bright young professional. The gay part wasn't in communication with those other parts. Of course I wondered if I was gay or maybe assumed I must be gay.

Were you in therapy during any of this time, or did you think you might have needed therapy?

I decided that psychoanalysis was the "best" therapy and did do that several times a week for several years. I later learned that this is the worst kind of therapy for people with trauma like mine—silence, no human contact really. But at that time, it was the gold standard. I think the therapy I needed wasn't really available then.

What happened with your family at that time?

My father had more heart attacks, and near the end we had a couple of weeks together while he was in the hospital. He had stopped drinking some time before and we actually had some good connection. He did apologize for the effect of his drinking on me, and it was kind of bittersweet. I wish I had had that father when I was growing up, not the one hidden behind the alcohol. That was our relationship when he died of another heart attack.

Meanwhile, my brother and I were trying to figure out how to deal with my mother, who was increasingly bizarre. He and his wife and kids moved onto the property where she lived and started hearing stories about "the crazy lady doctor." She had an improperly loaded shotgun that could have exploded anytime and once drove down the winding mountain roads at night with no lights, in reverse! She had asked some person passing by for sex. We decided she needed to be taken to the hospital for at least an evaluation.

I flew out and my mother got more and more suspicious about what her two sons were up to. She was drinking cheap jug wine, followed by vodka chasers, and she began to mumble her suspicions that we had arrived to steal all her money and possessions. She vowed, first thing in the morning, to drive to town and contact her attorneys to "kick us out of the will."

We had discreetly disabled both vehicles, so she flew into a rage and vowed to walk the many miles into town. I walked with her as she tried to push me off the high mountain roads down into the ravines. I must say, I was quite tempted to push her back. I knew the sheriff would arrive at some point because we had called him, and eventually he did and we got her into his car. Once she got to the hospital, it was awkward because the staff had all known her professionally.

Meanwhile, my brother and I went through the house. It was astounding: we found cases of alcohol stacked everywhere. Even more shocking was the hoard of self-prescribed medication. There were bottles in the medicine chest, the teapot, taped to the underside of the toilet bowl lid, in light fixtures, hidden behind the vents in the stone fireplaces, and tucked in between sheets and towels in the linen chest. We found some in the freezer, some in the refrigerator—just everywhere. My brother and I returned the following day with a full-size trash bag. There were some uppers, some downers, and who knows what else.

The diagnosis was that she had some form of viral brain disease and would not survive much longer. They helped us get legal guardianship of her. I was relieved that I could no longer be seen as the "evil son" who was out to get her.

All expectations were that she would not survive long, but she was moved to a good nursing facility where she lived for another 19 years. After a while I began to question the diagnosis and did some research. I suspected that she might have Alzheimer's, and after her death the autopsy confirmed that she had had Alzheimer's for many years. Things began to click and I realized she probably had the beginnings of it when I was in college or around that time. I recalled her secretary being extremely attentive and reminding "Dr. Ann" about everything she had to do or sign or attend. No wonder she had been able to function so well at work at the same time that she was increasingly irrational and strange when she was on her own.

How did you feel about her during all of this, once she was diagnosed and in a care facility?

I realized that I now had "the upper hand" and that I could have exacted revenge if I wanted to. But although it went through my mind, there wasn't much appeal. Ironically, I was now taking better care of her than she had ever taken of me.

What was the relationship like with your brother through all of this?

We were slowly finding some ground to stand on together. Not much, but a small bit. Then I got the news that he had committed suicide, leaving his wife and young children on their own. I was furious with him for doing it and bailing out on his responsibilities, and I also felt somehow like I should join him, as an act of solidarity. I was furious that the one person who shared a window with me into the past had removed himself. And I was angry that he had "caved" and let the perpetrators win. I was determined never to do that.

What did you do after your mother was living in the care facility and after your brother's suicide?

I came back to work and picked up where I left off. I tried living as a gay man for a while, but it didn't seem quite right. Eventually, I met a woman who seemed to like me, and we got to know each other very slowly over a long period of time and at some distances. I began to trust her and it was a very strange feeling. She knew everything about me, and I about her. She had her own problems and was accepting of mine. Although I had buried the memories of sexual abuse of any kind, she told me that I frequently brought up dreams about it, or mentioned it, all the while denying it.

We eventually married, but I knew there were more issues to be uncovered. She gently pointed out that I was drinking too much and I decided to stop. I didn't want to do what my parents had done, and I didn't want to give my stepson another alcoholic father. But without the alcohol, the memories started to come back. After I ended up in a dissociated child state, curled in a fetal position on our bed, I realized I needed a therapist.

How did you go about finding a therapist who could work with you since you weren't even sure what was going on with you at that point?

I fired one therapist and eventually found a woman very senior in the trauma community. She was used to what I was remembering and struggling with. I felt like I was going insane, while in fact, in many ways I was gradually inching towards sanity. That later became a bit of a slogan between my wife and me: that being insane was the easy part, the hard part was getting back to some kind of sanity.

I also have to emphasize that staying in the "forgetting" state was supported by working 80 hours a week, never getting exercise, having no safe space, and drinking. I had to cut down my work, find a safe space with my wife, and take care of myself somewhat, before the memories started to return.

How did you discover the multiple "people" in your personality, and how did you work with them?

First, my talk therapist and I gradually realized there were really several personalities present. We made a kind of chart and tried to name and identify every part, and then every day I would try to check in with all the parts. I journaled a huge amount and tried to be more conscious of how I shifted from one to the other, and what feelings they all had. Each part carried its own feelings, separate from the others. It was essential to keep making a safe place inside myself, inside my life, as well as in my therapy.

Did you work mostly with this individual therapist?

She's always been my main therapist, and we've used EMDR and other approaches. I've also done a lot of groups, where people get it when you talk about emotional abuse and sexual abuse. I was in a retreat with 45 other men, and the leader asked how many of us had been sexually abused by a female and over 20 of us raised our hands. That was profound. Some of the group work was in this kind of intensive weekend workshop, which I've attended for years.

I also did a substantial amount of body work, with two different men. Because of that work, for years, I finally feel I actually live in my body, which I didn't do for over 50 years.

One thing happened that probably validated my own experience and helped me understand the bigger picture. After my brother committed suicide, his daughters started reporting strange dreams and images of somebody coming into their bedrooms at night and touching their legs and their genitals, all in silence and while they were supposedly asleep. It seemed obvious to me that my brother had done that to them and that our mother had abused both of us in the same bizarre way. After all, both of us had those flimsy unlockable bedroom doors. The girls never outright accused my brother of abuse, but I felt I was certain about what had happened. I also suspect that his guilt about that played a role in his suicide.

My wife and I are also involved in an organization that uses some of the 12-step ideas to heal from sexual abuse. We've changed a lot of the language and ideas, but that's where we started. We continue to work on our own issues and offer help to others.

Where are you now in this journey?

A while back I was driving along in my car, and I was trying to think of some of my various personalities and I couldn't get a sense of "them." I had more of a sense of "me" and I realize parts of me had spontaneously integrated. I was so stunned I just pulled over to the side of the road. I felt a sense of great and profound serenity and a sense of sadness. I sat with both states. The sadness waned; the serenity remains a touchstone that I can, and do, return to.

The last time my therapist and I discussed my going to another weekend intensive, we decided that maybe it was time to take a workshop in photography instead. So the reparative process is finally beginning to wind down, and I'm mostly integrated in a way that feels healthy and good.

What's been the most helpful to you?

Continuing to shelter and then grow a sense of self-respect and self-love and self-awareness, probably "mirrored" for me by the Hopi housekeepers. I only had them for a few years, but their unconditional love and protection were invaluable.

I've also had a drive to heal, to *not* let the predators in my childhood win. I think that started when part of me realized I had to go far away to survive. One of my personalities was totally focused on planning my escape.

At this point I also have a sense of compassion, if not forgiveness, for the complex lives my parents and brother lived. Theirs was an arid emotional desert; I now live in a garden.

RANDALL'S STORY: MY REFLECTIONS

It's quite unusual for a person with this diagnosis—DID—to sustain the level of professional achievement that Randall did, as well as sustaining a healthy and loving marriage. He had periods of deep dysfunction, but partly because of the DID he was able to continue working and "passing" as someone in control of his life. The DID in some sense protected him even in adulthood, and by the time it started to come apart as a defense, he was established enough to weather those storms.

His resilience seems to have come from a couple of places: first, the "seed corn" of early maternal care from his Hopi caregivers, and second, his intellect as well as a drive to succeed and to leave his family. He recognized early that he needed to escape and was able to plan that in a healthy and socially acceptable way.

Unlike many of the other men in this book, he seems to have little or no sense of being bad, guilty, or responsible for the horrific treatment he received. It may be that his early caregiving was able to give him a solid inner core of feeling that he was a "good boy," which was not dislodged by maternal rejection, rage, contempt, and abuse.

Randall has put more work into recovery than most, and the benefits have been remarkable.

WHAT CAN WE LEARN FROM RANDALL'S STORY?

Finding the right therapists has been key for him, and he's successfully combined talk therapy, body therapy, and group therapy as well as support groups and weekend intensives. Most trauma experts agree that severely traumatized people need several modes of treatment and they often recommend talk therapy, bodywork of some kind, meditation or mindfulness training, and group work. I would also add that most need some kind of creative place in which to express things via art, poetry, writing, dance—anything that taps into a place of freedom and creativity.

Randall describes and details his overall therapy very well, and in fact his story was included in one of his therapist's books about body trauma and healing. For purposes of this book, his healing journey has been shortened considerably, and I've encouraged him to do some of his own writing on this topic.

12

Christopher: "I should have been able to save her"

This last chapter is not an interview but rather the story of my older brother's life before he committed suicide in his mid-40s. He left behind a manuscript/ autobiography that he wrote a few years before his death, but he wrote only about his life from his childhood until about the time he graduated from college. I think it paints a picture of his life that explains a lot about his death. I saw this manuscript for the first time about two years ago. Here is his story, in his own words.

It seems strange that during the 40 years of my life I have never been requested to write an autobiography before. I approach this task with a considerable degree of dread, apprehension, and trepidation. Part of this irrational fear originates from a concern that my psychiatrist may reject me after discovering what a failure I've been. Another fear is that I may reject myself even more after scrutinizing my past in black and white and realizing what things could have been, but never were.

Although I consider my life in many ways a failure, as I sit here writing it is with a copy of my curriculum vitae in a folder, and I cannot help noticing that I received a fellowship to complete my psychiatric residency at Harvard Medical School and that I was asked to remain on the faculty for several years after that, teaching part-time at Harvard in addition to my private practice and my job as a psychiatrist in a state hospital. Other achievements look equally satisfactory. I find it extremely difficult to reconcile this factual material about my life and integrate it into my feelings about my life. My feeling is that, up to this point, I have accomplished nothing.

Viewed by a stranger, my life would look successful. I am happily married to a marvelous, unusual lady who gives me all the love and understanding any husband could desire. We have two lovely children who would be the envy of any parents. From all outward appearances, it would appear that I'm successful, yet this idea is totally foreign to my mind.

Another concern I have about writing is that, since I feel I have accomplished nothing so far, I'll see how bleak my future looks. What do the next 40 years look like—if I make it?

I'll begin with my childhood, although I know it can only be incomplete. I have vivid memories extending back to a very early age, but there's much more I don't know. I was born in Chicago, as my parents' first child. Evidently my mother's pregnancy and delivery were normal. My father was just finishing his medical residency at the University of Chicago, and residents barely scraped by financially in those days. They lived in a small apartment, in a building with other medical residents and their families.

I feel both my parents loved me a great deal during my early childhood, although later on my father became competitive with me, and my mother became suspicious of me due to emotional problems. I was always told I was an extremely curious and imaginative child, and for a long period of time my mother alluded to a "special relationship" she had with me due to my being her first child.

One of my early memories is being frightened of company and people who would come to the house. My parents made me come out and meet company they had, shake hands with them, and kiss people goodnight that I didn't know or trust.

When I was about two years old, my brother David was born. He had colic and was quite a difficult child for his first year of life. My mother felt she couldn't comfort him, and he did cry a lot, as I recall. When he was about a year old, we moved to Oklahoma City where my father was the youngest chairman of a medical school department of pathology in the United States. This was quite an honor. When we made the trip there from Chicago we traveled by train, and I didn't realize my father wasn't coming on the train with my mother and brother and me, as he had work to finish in Chicago. I was horrified to see him standing on the platform, waving, as our train pulled out of the station. I thought he had been left behind for good.

Thing were uneventful for some time. My mother seemed fine; my father was busy at work, and my younger sister Susan was born, so we were a family of five. I recall my father stating on several occasions,

"I think our boy is a genius," referring to my interest in mechanical devices and the fact that I took them apart and put them back together endlessly. I was always treated as a "genius" by my parents, while my younger siblings were not.

My life was shattered at the age of six. One of my most vivid memories was that horrible day when my mother became psychotic. She had often been sad before and frequently cried at home when my father was away. She used to cry on my shoulder when I barely came up to her waist. In retrospect, I feel that if I had only done or said the right thing perhaps I could have saved my mother. I know these feelings sound ridiculous, and the notion of a six-year-old boy saving his mother from a major psychiatric illness sounds preposterous, but nevertheless that is the way I feel. Somehow I feel that my mother would not have come to me seeking advice if I had not been able to give advice. Somehow I failed her in a very tragic way.

On the day things really got bad, I was supposed to have a report card from first grade signed by my mother and then take it to school for the teacher's inspection. My mother was in a peculiar psychotic state in which she was unable to move. She stayed in one position and could not or would not speak to me and could not move her body. I was terrified and knew nothing about what I later learned, that it is called a catatonic state. I went to school without my report card being signed and was obviously very upset. When I returned from school my mother had been taken away, I later learned, to the psychiatric ward of the general hospital.

She remained there for about three weeks, and my memories are all tangled up at this point. I do not remember ever being told what was wrong and certainly did not understand what was wrong with her. Later on I learned that she had been given electroshock treatment and that she had also been extremely depressed.

When she returned home, it seemed as if she was no longer my mother. I am unable to express how important this occurrence is in my life. It is difficult for you or anyone to imagine the impact on a small child of seeing his mother in such a bizarre state, then having her taken away for a lengthy period of time with no understanding of what the problem was.

Nevertheless, I believe the most traumatic part was when she returned. When she returned she was not my mother. I vividly recall feeling that my real mother had never come back from the hospital. The mother that did come back spoke very slowly and had a monotonous voice. She seemed like "death warmed over." I recall later in my life feeling that it might have been better for my mother to die, disappear forever, than come back seemingly a different person.

After this event she never seemed to be the same to me again, although I gradually got used to her. She seemed to lack the vivaciousness she once had, as well as the spontaneity and self-esteem. She seemed unsure of everything she did and had a great deal of difficulty asserting herself with my father. Whenever she seemed to get upset with my father he always attributed it to "her illness," and it seems to me he used this as an excuse for failing to give full credence to the normal concerns and problems that arise between two spouses.

One day I recall very vividly that she got in an argument with my father over something having to do with disciplining the children, and my father took the three of us into another room and explained to us that my mother was "sick and mentally ill." My mother overheard the conversation in the other room and started crying and thrashing around. Later on I understood much better what impact it must have had on her to hear her children being told that she was an "incomplete mother."

My mother and father used to argue quietly but with a lot of tension at the dinner table and all of the children would join in. Apparently, there were many problems having to do with disciplining the children. My mother began to drink more and more heavily until she reached the point of alcoholism, hiding alcohol and consuming too much on a daily basis. My father's reaction was to work longer hours, coming home late in the evening.

No story of my life could be complete without mention of Sarah, our black "maid." She meant a great deal to all of us and was the perfect image of a "black nanny." She was a large woman who came to take care of us and do the housework several days a week. Although in some ways she was a no-nonsense caretaker, she was also very caring and as devoted to us as we were to her. I don't believe my mother could have ever survived without Sarah's help and overseeing of the house and children. In many times of personal stress I went to Sarah with my problems, and she was always willing to comfort me and offer practical advice.

I recall few friends except for my first girlfriend, whom I was obsessed with for a long time. I was very shy and didn't kiss a girl until I was in college. As for schoolwork, I studied hard and got good grades; but although my parents considered me a "genius," I have now come to realize that my performance was not as outstanding as I was led to believe. I was always several years ahead of my schoolmates in reading and math but didn't actually fall in the "genius" range, although I had plenty of nurturance and help available at home. I always felt I did not live up to my father's view of me as a "genius," and objective tests showed I was very bright, but that was all. Although the reader may not appreciate this distinction, it is a very important one to me.

I had few friends and was considered the "odd ball" of the class. I was almost always the tallest boy in the class but never participated in sports. My father considerably de-emphasized sports, and later I learned that one of his legs had been affected by childhood polio and that he was unable to do much strenuous physical activity after that. For me, school was drudgery and my good grades were not much of a reward. I was extremely shy and self-conscious, and if I was ever invited to a party, it was more of an ordeal than a place to have any fun.

ABOUT THE FAMILY

My mother was the older of two girls in a family in which she felt pressured by her own mother to be more pliable, rather than the curious, intelligent girl that she was. Her younger sister was beautiful and submissive, and soon outshone my mother in her parents' eyes. My mother did well in school and was outstanding as a college student, evidently free from emotional problems at that time. She was seen as truly gifted and had a close circle of women friends, all of whom achieved public acclaim in writing, in American Indian anthropology, and in art and sculpture. My mother was the only one of these women who became ill, and never lived up to the potential she evidently had.

Her first psychotic break was, as I described, when I was 6 and she was 36. She may have had some early warning signs a few years prior, but information about that is spotty. In the next section of this paper, I'll write more about what happened later on.

My father has always been a very hard worker, and he himself says that his accomplishments should be credited to hard work and not to great intellectual gifts. He has had prestigious jobs in various medical schools, received many awards for his work, and has written many books and countless articles. He spent much time at work, and seemed unavailable to me as a father. I do not feel that he was a very effective role model for me, nor did I feel that I could ever go to him with my problems. He was completely divorced from any emotional aspects of his life and still is. I feel that he devotes a tremendous amount of energy to keep himself from experiencing his feelings. I'm sure he considers me a failure.

Nevertheless, when I was much younger he used to spend a fair amount of time with me, when he had the time. I recall that he had a consulting job many hours away from his work, and that he would take me there on occasion, and we would talk about many things on the way. He bought me my first microscope, but while I wanted to have some fun with it and look at all kinds of things, he insisted that I get three-by-five cards and classify everything I looked at according to a book on taxonomy which was for college students. (I was 12 at the time.)

He must have had an inkling of the marital problems he and my mother had, because he used to ask me to rate their marriage on a scale of 1 to 10, based on what I saw in other households. I really had no idea of what he was talking about and I think I always gave him a "10." He wanted me to go into pathology—his field—and it was hard to switch from that to psychiatry, a field that he dislikes. I believe some psychiatrists he and my mother consulted over the years told him he was out of touch with his feelings and that it was contributing to the marital problems, and he certainly did not want to hear that feedback. I went into psychiatry partly to help people like my mother, and to better understand myself as well.

Although I am closer to my younger brother David than anyone else, we developed sibling rivalry, which in retrospect I think made life difficult for him. My excelling at school was held up to him in some way, and he had more difficulty at school and more trouble deciding what he wanted to do, until finally excelling in his chosen field of veterinary medicine. Although I feel close to him, we have probably never completely reconciled all these parts of our relationship.

My sister and I are further apart in age and were not close growing up. She was closer to our middle brother, and they had friends and playmates in our neighborhood, while I was more focused on my studies and science activities. Interestingly enough, she also went into the field of mental health. We've had limited contact since becoming adults, although we visit back and forth occasionally.

There were few happy days during my adolescence. I didn't know what to do with my sexual feelings, and my parents were too old-fashioned to do more than the minimal awkward explanations about sex. I know my father wanted me to remain focused on my studies and not to be distracted by teenage concerns. Between that, my glasses, acne, and short haircut, I was not popular with the girls and was still extremely shy in social situations. I did not partake of any of the "adolescent rebellion" to which people often refer. I was considered very naïve by my fellow students and was the target of many jokes as a result. I performed poorly in gym class, because of lack of encouragement and generally being uncoordinated. I was sent to some camps during the summers, but became homesick and felt like an outsider. It seemed I couldn't do things right and that people laughed at me. I focused on my studies and substituted getting along with my teachers and mentors for getting along with my peers.

When I was 13, my father received a Fulbright Fellowship to take the entire family to New Zealand for a year and for him to teach at the University of Dunedin there. This is one of the few really happy experiences I remember. We had fun on the ship voyage of three weeks, and played games and made friends with other kids our age. Once we arrived and were settled in, it seemed to me that my schoolmates made an effort to get to know me and befriend me. I really was an "outsider"—an American—and perhaps that made things better for once.

When we returned to the States, my father wanted the family to move to another state where we could live on a farm—or at least in a rural location, as he had when he was a child. My mother had a number of close friends and family in Oklahoma City where we lived, and she was tearful at the prospect of leaving. I'll never forget what I term "the infamous vote" which my father took in order to force my mother to move. He decided that everyone should have an equal vote about staying or moving, then made sure that all the children understood that they would be able to ride horses and have a wonderful time in the new location. Needless to say, the "vote" was 4 against 1, with the children being in the awkward position of voting against their mother. My mother was upset and tearful and clearly unable to assert herself.

The move was, in retrospect, disastrous. My mother had another serious breakdown. In addition to becoming an even worse alcoholic, she became extremely depressed and bizarre in her actions. She was hospitalized again and again received electroshock treatment as well as medications. I learned later that much or all of this was apparently against her will, or at least she felt it was against her will. She never seemed quite right after this episode, becoming more of an automaton and more forgetful. She didn't seem anything like the bright, creative, spontaneous person I had known as a young child, but seemed to be "waiting out her days."

I remember being very sensitive to her problems at this time, although I was never kept informed about exactly what they were. I suppose I felt somewhat responsible for what happened to her because she still tended to come to me when things became very difficult. It was during this time that I began to have the idea that "if all else failed," I could go into psychiatry. This had to represent the "end of the line" for me due to the fact that my father was so opposed to the field and wanted me to go into another branch of medicine. Because of my father's very overwhelming personality, I believe that I had to think of psychiatry as a career in these terms—"if all else failed."

To go back to high school days, I took the college entrance exams early and could have gone to college two years early, except for my mother's strenuous objection. I did go one year early. Although I scored very high on the achievement tests, the scores were certainly not in the "genius" range at all, as were the scores of many of my classmates at Swarthmore College, where I went. I was someone of above-average intelligence who had worked hard to be an early achiever. My social skills were woefully lacking. What had been accomplished was out of extreme sacrifice, although I was too young to know everything I had sacrificed at that time.

My summers during my high school years were also times of high pressure and high expectation. My father always arranged some sort of research fellowship student position for me, usually with one of his renowned colleagues. Although it is easy to see that this could have been a wonderful opportunity, I was weighed down with the expectation of being some phenomenal student, and hid from other people while spending almost all my time trying to live up to this. I had and still have a terrible fear of being "found out." Weekends were spent studying while the other summer interns were out having a good time. I was terribly lonely and isolated and look back now with some bitterness that my father pushed me into the morass of academia because he was doing the only thing he knew how to do.

Swarthmore College was very expensive, and it was a sacrifice for my father to send me there. I know he wanted the best for me, and that as an only child himself, he wanted to make sure I had the opportunities he never had. Once I arrived, my fears were realized, because many of my peers were in fact "geniuses" or close to it, and equally hardworking as I was. I struggled to make C's in most of my courses. I had some moderate depression at that time, having difficulty sleeping and difficulty getting going in the mornings. I probably needed an antidepressant at that time, and something to help me with my extreme anxiety before exams.

I recall with some bitterness that Swarthmore had no student health program that included any type of psychological counseling, and that a number of suicides were committed on the campus. I am able to express bitter feelings about this and feel that a school exerting pressure of this magnitude upon its students should make psychological help available. For this reason I have never made a financial contribution of any kind since graduating, and have never attended a class reunion.

At the beginning of my junior year, I developed a moderately serious depression and made the decision that I simply did not want to return to college, although I didn't know what else I should do. My father talked to me a lot, but we never sought professional advice. I had very negative feelings about myself and confessed to him my almost total lack of a social life. In the end, I returned to college and was put in a program for "self-motivated" students. This was ideal for me because I could spend all my time studying, basically giving up the idea of having a social life at all. I did find a girlfriend, an extremely shy girl who was attractive and who liked me, and I felt better than I had in a long time.

I finally did graduate, with the lowest level of honors. That was an achievement, but again, not the stellar achievement which I was supposed to deliver. I had been accepted into medical school, but for once, my father thought I should have a summer "off" traveling in Europe with the Youth Hostel Organization. It was a summer of pure fun for me, and I wish he had seen and encouraged the value of this kind of thing before I had graduated from college. I became close friends with some of the other hostellers, and got in good shape by bicycling long distances. We traveled everywhere and had great adventures.

* * *

My brother's autobiography ends here, at the age of 20, although he wrote it at 40. Drawing from other sources—my own memories and those of my brother David, and extensive conversation with Chris's widow—I can fill in some of what happened from our vantage points during those years, until the time of his death.

Chris graduated from medical school and pursued psychiatry, doing well enough to be invited to teach some basic courses at Harvard. During medical school, which he found quite difficult, he happened on the kinds of chemical aids that many medical students, interns, and residents use to stay awake, study, and perform. He began to take amphetamines and sleeping pills, and once he could prescribe medicine, it seems he began a long stint of prescribing various psychotropic meds for himself. Later on, ironically, he was seen as an excellent medication consultant.

He married, then divorced after about 10 years, partly over his wish to have a child and his wife's concerns about his alcohol and medication intake. All this is to say he continued using all kinds of substances to manage his moods and his ongoing sense of inadequacy.

He married again, a Mormon woman with a son from a prior marriage; the father had left the family some years earlier. Chris adopted this delightful young boy, and both enjoyed the father-son relationship. They lived in Utah, and Chris found a job at a state hospital, where again he seemed to do well. He became involved in the church and seemed to buy into the beliefs, which he writes about in notebooks he kept in the last few years of his life. He and his wife, a calm, sane woman and an excellent mother with a great deal of patience, had a daughter after a few years, and it soon became evident that the little girl had some major problems. Her diagnosis is unclear, but she has some form of retardation, and is cognitively and emotionally on the level of a six- or seven-year-old child, with a sweet disposition and a friendly, sociable nature.

My brother was very thrown by this, feeling once again he had failed in some way by producing an "inferior" child. He felt that our father confirmed this assessment, since he had little to no interest in spending any time with this grandchild or getting to know her. (However, our father also showed little to no interest in his son David's daughter, who recently completed graduate school at Harvard, so his disinterest clearly was not limited to "inferior" children.)

From that time on, Chris continued to deteriorate at home, although he did well at work. His notebooks are filled with obsessive observations about the effect of each of many medications that he took each day. He experimented with a wide range of drugs over the course of many years, ranging from lithium to MAO inhibitors to amphetamines to Haldol, just to name a few. He diagnosed himself as bipolar at one point, and his notebooks record his fears of an underlying psychotic disorder despite no evidence of that. According to his widow, he was always fearful of becoming schizophrenic well past the age our mother developed symptoms and even further past the usual age of onset for men (late teens or early 20s).

These same notebooks contain reflections about his ongoing therapy and his thoughts about his own condition. They also contain thoughts about his responsibility for our mother and his fears that he was much like her in his problems with alcohol, his tendency toward depression, and his hopelessness about relating well to his children. One direct quote from a notebook less than a year before his suicide: "I feel I deeply harmed my mother as a child, making her depressed and making her go to the hospital." There are a number of notations about a recurrence of thoughts of suicide, and decisions—never carried out—that he should get rid of his gun collection.

Despite his guilt about our mother, he was avoidant in the extreme when visiting her. His widow told me: "There was the time we went to Washington, DC, for a psychiatric convention, and it was the first time I had met your mother and of course it was the worst time. She was not coping very well, her apartment was a mess, and she had accidentally turned off her refrigerator and so the apartment was in horrific condition. I remember thinking it quite odd how Chris reacted to the whole thing: pretty much avoidance. He definitely did not want to deal with it. He begged me to take care of it while he attended his meetings, so I spent three or four days cleaning up and getting to know your mom.

"During that entire week Chris was acting very strange. He was taking amphetamines along with his regular antidepressants and then he began taking some kind of 'natural' antidepressant pills because he read an article in the *New England Journal of Medicine* that they enhanced moods. I can't remember what they were, but you were not supposed to take them with MAO inhibitors and of course he wasn't supposed to drink alcohol either, but Chris did both. He ended up being pretty much totally out of it and missed most of his meetings. He slept for most of the days in our hotel room. I felt the whole overmedicating thing was partly to avoid dealing with your mom.

"Chris was quite angry about your mother being given ECT when he was a young child, and again a few years later. He felt it harmed her irreparably and that your father never should have allowed it. Although he understood ECT and its potentially good effects, he was very leery of it."

He was eventually hospitalized in a psychiatric hospital for impaired physicians, with a diagnosis of depression, and stayed there for several weeks. Five months later, he was hospitalized again. This time, there was a new plan: to take him off all medications for a few weeks, in order to assess him without anything in his system. If he became depressed again, the plan was to try ECT.

He knew that his wife was planning to take the kids to her mother's for a while, a few hundred miles away, because they were having a hard time with his moods and his hospitalizations. He knew his job was waiting for him. But at some point, he got a one-hour pass from the locked ward in the hospital, and the next news anyone had of him was from the police, 18 hours later, saying that his body had been found in a motel room. He had purchased and concealed a gun and used it to commit suicide. He did not leave a note and there were no drugs or alcohol in his system.

Our family is left with the question all families of suicides are left with: why? The best we pieced together was that Chris felt extremely and irrationally guilty that he had not been able to "save" our mother, and was also horrified at the possibility of ending up like her. Facing ECT, which he felt left her in a state no better than dead, and feeling that perhaps it was his fault in the first place, I believe he simply couldn't face what he was sure his future held and saw no other way to escape either his guilt or his fear. It was a potent, and lethal, combination.

After Chris's death, both parents declined: my mother mentally, my father physically. Although both of them outlived him by more than a decade, none of us has truly outlived his suicide. I consider it not only a legacy of our family and our life together but also a legacy of the stigma and silence surrounding mental illness.

As with the other men whose stories you are reading, I'll ask the question: what would have helped? If someone had intervened early, when our mother was first sick, and told Chris in particular that her illness was not his fault and above all that he could not fix it, I think it might have helped. If her illness had been treated as an illness and not a dark secret, we all would have been better off. He "knew" as much as anyone could know, intellectually, once he was an adult, but the deeper thought, etched into his child's mind with nothing to contradict it, was that he should have been able to save her.

One last note: My brother's story of his family is not quite the same as *my* story of our family. Oddly enough, I have no recollection of thinking he was a genius and had no idea until I read his autobiography that he lived with that burden. Some of the events he recounts I remember in just the same way; others I remember very differently. He leaves out some things that were important to me. Being several years younger, I didn't know the mother he knew, and being both a youngest and a girl, I had a completely different relationship with our father.

I do know that it always made a deep impression on me that he was named not just Christopher, but Christopher Robin, after our parents' favorite children's books. That seemed to me burden enough for any child. In the books, Christopher Robin has all the answers; he's the one all the characters in the stories go to when they're stumped by a problem. He always finds a way to fix things and to cheer everyone up. Christopher Robin is the one who's supposed to save everyone.

13

Conclusions

Now that you've read these stories, you have some sense of the challenges of growing up with a mentally ill parent. In each story, whether dramatic or subtle, the shadow of both the illness and the stigma fell over the whole family. Stigma and shame added unnecessary suffering to the burden of learning how to cope with these illnesses, already devastating enough in their own right.

This book contains the stories of 12 men, so it's a start, but we need to hear from more men with more diverse experiences. We also need to pay attention to the growing body of evidence about how to strengthen children's resilience and how to continue to reduce the stigma around mental illnesses.

HOW ARE BOYS LIKELY TO BE AFFECTED BY GROWING UP WITH A MENTALLY ILL PARENT?

Recent research shows that boys are more sensitive and more emotionally reactive than girls, running counter to our stereotype of boys being tougher or less affected by emotional stressors. Infant boys generally cry more, are more fussy, are harder to soothe, and take more of their mother's (or primary caregiver's) time and energy, face-to-face, to settle down after upset. They are more vulnerable to separations and disruptions in their relationships with their mothers and generally require more help and support learning to manage and regulate their emotions.[1]

If a mother (or primary attachment figure) of a very young child becomes ill, that child is very distressed, but it might be somewhat harder on a young boy than a young girl. When it's the father who is ill, the results seem to show up a little later in boys: the men in this book felt sad about not having a male role model and knew that even as adults they sought and needed a lot of approval from older males, sometimes to their own detriment.

This important research on boys and their emotional development is relatively new and will hopefully change some of our expectations of boys as they grow up. We've been accustomed to raising boys to show strength, toughness, and emotional resilience before they are even old enough to have developed these emotional capabilities. It's as though we're expecting boys to walk (emotionally) before they even know how to crawl. As it is, boys are often shamed into suppressing their fears, hurts, and confusions, leaving them even more vulnerable. Men are taught that it's weak to even have these feelings, much less express them. We also raise boys to feel responsible for fixing things, whether the thing needing fixing is a broken toy or a broken parent.[2]

Research would suggest, then, that a boy has a harder time getting his bearings when a parent changes dramatically, or even disappears, as parents often do when they are mentally ill. It's frightening and confusing for all children, and if we discourage boys from showing their distress, we may miss the signals that they need help. Our expectations may be higher for boys, while in fact their ability to cope with distress is less well developed than we have realized.

IS THERE A DIFFERENCE BETWEEN MEN AND WOMEN WHO GREW UP WITH A MENTALLY ILL PARENT?

I found a fascinating difference between the men in this book and the women in *Daughters of Madness*. Despite some real horror stories about their early experiences, almost every one of the 20 women asked me at some point, "Was it really that bad?" They needed my authoritative reassurance that yes, their story was really "that bad." They all seemed to question their own assessment of what had happened to them. And that uncertainty persisted into adulthood, as they also questioned their ability to "read" other people emotionally and to accurately assess the meaning of emotional encounters. Their emotional compass didn't feel reliable to them.

In contrast, not a single one of the men asked me that question. None of the men seemed to doubt themselves in the way that all the women did.

They were sure of what happened, and they were sure of how "bad" it was, even without much outside validation. What the men *did* question, almost across the board, was first, whether they should have been able to shrug it off and second, whether they should have been able to fix it.

Although they knew that a child couldn't really fix a sick parent, some of these men still carried guilt and a sense of inadequacy because they felt they had failed. More than one boy cleaned house, cooked meals, brought cold cloths for Mom's headaches, or tried to entertain her and cheer her up. Some of the men seemed to feel "stupid" even telling me about these things, exposing their childish efforts, hopes, and dreams. That feeling of embarrassment told me that they still harbored some of those hopes and still thought of themselves as failures.

WHAT REALLY HELPS A CHILD WHO IS GROWING UP WITH A MENTALLY ILL PARENT?

The answers to this question are always the same. All the men and women I interviewed, and all the at-risk children of mentally ill parents questioned by researchers in various studies, gave the same answers about what helps. These answers are simple and indisputable; there's no reason to make it more complicated or to think we need more research to verify it. Here are the answers, in their own voices:

> "It would have helped if someone had explained what was going on."
>
> "It would have helped if I knew it wasn't my fault."
>
> "It would have helped if I knew it wasn't up to me to fix it."
>
> "It would have helped if someone could have listened to me about what it was like for me to have a mom or dad who was different."
>
> "It would have helped to be able to talk about it like other kids talked about what was going on in their families."
>
> "It would have helped if other people knew more about mental illness so it wouldn't seem so weird and scary to them."

When children have these resources, they can develop very high levels of psychological resilience using their native intelligence, humor, and imagination. When they're kept in the dark, struggling with confusion, isolation, and shame, all of their energy goes into simply surviving something they don't even understand.

WHAT MAKES THE STIGMA SO BAD? IT'S UNCOMFORTABLE BUT IS IT REALLY DESTRUCTIVE?

Stigma does more than bring unearned shame to people who have done nothing to be ashamed of. The shame associated with stigma also means silence, ignorance, and fear. Family members often don't even talk to each other about a stigma that touches them all. It's like a huge cloud of "don't ask, don't tell," which inevitably means less knowledge, less understanding, and more difficulty just coping. As we just saw in the list of "what would make it better," all the answers have to do with openness, free communication, and understanding. Yes, it's uncomfortable to be stigmatized, but it doesn't end there.

Years ago, cancer used to be highly stigmatized: nobody talked about it, people who disclosed that they had cancer found to their dismay that they were virtually shunned, and most of us had little accurate information. We thought of it as "the big C" and we "knew" it was a death sentence. We didn't realize that people all around us might have had cancer, because they didn't talk about it. Now we deal with cancer in a completely different way. Yes, it's still a tough disease; but because it's out in the open and people talk about it, we know more about it and can ask questions, get information, and be helpful to the people we know who are diagnosed with it. If we are diagnosed, we don't fear being shunned and isolated. In fact, we might invite our friends to a "cancer awareness" fund-raiser. We look back at our past attitudes as being from the Dark Ages, but we're the same way now about mental illnesses.

We would be horrified to think that a young child would feel responsible for causing his or her mother or father's cancer and responsible for curing it. We would want to reassure the child that cancer is a disease and that nothing the child did caused it and that the child wasn't responsible for curing it. We would want to tell the child that he or she can help out and be part of the family team, but it is up to the doctor to help Mom or Dad get well again.

Our silence around mental illness means that many children believe that they caused their parent's illness and that it's up to them to cure it. Young children are not psychologically mature enough to realize that they are not the cause of everything that happens around them; children will automatically assume that something is their fault unless an adult tells them otherwise. And what children believe early on can be like a handprint in wet cement; once it dries, it's very hard to undo. That's why it's so important to be open and informative with children early and, often, not waiting until they're "old enough to understand."

Children are masters at picking up subtle changes in their parents, and masters at pretending to be okay because they don't want to upset their parents. It is simply not true that "the kids are fine" without information and inclusion in something as huge as a major illness in one of their parents.

For men, the stigma about mental illness, the "man code" of emotional toughness, and the reality of having a mentally ill parent create a pressure cooker of conflicting needs that can be overwhelming. First, a mentally ill parent's illness almost always causes distress, confusion, fear, loss, and helplessness. Second, the stigma around mental illnesses means that children are less likely to ask questions inside or outside the family, and adults are less likely to offer information; the family is more likely to be isolated, and the general unspoken message is "this is so awful we can't even notice it and talk about it." Third, we encourage and expect boys and men to be emotionally tough in a way that makes it even harder for boys to ask for help.

Children who carry this kind of guilt and responsibility can be burdened for life with those feelings. In this book, Chris and Tim are two such children. Chris formed the idea as a child that he was responsible for his mother's psychosis and that he should make her well. Even as an adult, and a psychiatrist who "knew better," this belief was still etched in his mind. His failure to cure his mother, and his guilt about it, were part of what led to his suicide, according to his own journals.

Tim was indirectly and directly blamed and burdened with his mother's illness numerous times. His father simply left the kids to take care of their suicidal mother, and his mother railed against her children for "not loving her." To this day Tim carries a kind of survivor guilt that may be compromising his ability to thrive in his own life.

In contrast, David was reassured in the simplest possible way about his severely ill mother when his father prayed nightly, "God help Mommy to get well." It was an open acknowledgment that something was wrong and could be noticed and talked about. And as David said, "If Mommy was sick, then she could get well."

Thomas talked freely about his mother's illness, even explaining everything to his friends when they saw his mother "being stretchered out of the house." Thomas was even told what was wrong and why it happened, and he was offered lengthy family therapy and the freedom to talk, to rage, and to cry. Despite serious and very disruptive mental illnesses in their midst, David and Thomas suffered the least from stigma and guilt, and both are doing very well.

I wouldn't like being held responsible for something that was totally out of my control. I don't think anyone would like it. But this is the burden we leave children with when we don't talk honestly to them about a serious illness in a parent they love. Children want to help, they want to make their parents happy, and they don't have much ability on their own to figure out what they can do and what they can't. It's up to the adults to tell them: you're a child; you didn't cause this and you can't fix it, but you can help out. It's okay to ask questions and to ask for help. It's okay to keep living your life as a child, without picking up a burden of guilt and failure about something that has nothing to do with guilt and failure.

I hope that this book moves us even just a tiny bit toward knowing more, a place of more concern and acceptance rather than fear and ignorance. Stigma doesn't thrive in the full light of day; I'd like to think stories like these shine a little light into some dark and lonely places.

NOTES

1. M. Katherine Weinberg, Edward Tronick, Jeffrey F. Cohn, and Karen C. Olsen, "Gender Differences in Emotional Expressivity and Self-Regulation during Early Infancy," *Developmental Psychology* 35 (1999): 175–88.

2. William Pollack, *Real Boys: Rescuing Our Sons from the Myths of Boyhood* (New York: Holt, 1998).

Suggested Reading

Alda, Alan. *Never Have Your Dog Stuffed*. New York: Random House, 2005.

Beardslee, William R. *Out of the Darkened Room: When a Parent Is Depressed: Protecting the Children and Strengthening the Family*. Boston: Little, Brown, 2002.

Burroughs, Augusten. *Running with Scissors*. New York: St. Martin's Press, 2002.

Hinshaw, Stephen P. *Breaking the Silence: Mental Health Professionals Disclose Their Personal and Family Experience of Mental Illness*. Oxford: Oxford University Press, 2008.

Hinshaw, Stephen P. *The Years of Silence Are Past: My Father's Life with Bipolar Disorder*. Cambridge: Cambridge University Press, 2002.

Kimmel, Michael. *Guyland: The Perilous World Where Boys Become Men*. New York: HarperCollins, 2008.

Pollack, William. *Real Boys: Rescuing Our Sons from the Myths of Boyhood*. New York: Holt, 1998.

Way, Niobe. *Deep Secrets: Boy's Friendships and the Crisis of Connection*. Cambridge, MA: Harvard University Press, 2011.

Index

About the Author

Susan L. Nathiel, PhD, is a psychotherapist in private practice in Hamden, Connecticut. She has been in practice for over 35 years seeing individuals, couples, and families. She is the author of *Daughters of Madness: Growing Up and Older with a Mentally Ill Mother* (Praeger, 2007).